THE TECH SET

Ellyssa Kroski, Series Editor

Location-Aware Services and QR Codes for Libraries

Joe Murphy

ALA TechSource

An imprint of the American Library Association

Chicago   2012

Printed in the United States of America

Library of Congress Control Number: 2012009039

ISBN: 978-1-55570-784-2

♾ This paper meets the requirements of ANSI/NISO Z39.48-1992 (Permanence of Paper).

CONTENTS

Foreword *by Ellyssa Kroski* . . . .　v

Preface . . . .　ix

1. Introduction . . . .　1

2. Types of Solutions Available . . . .　9

3. Planning . . . .　19

4. Social Mechanics . . . .　25

5. Implementation . . . .　29

6. Marketing . . . .　81

7. Best Practices . . . .　89

8. Metrics . . . .　95

9. Developing Trends . . . .　101

Recommended Reading . . . .　107

Index . . . .　109

About the Author . . . .　116

Don't miss this book's companion website!

Turn the page for details.

THE TECH SET® Volumes 11–20 is more than just the book you're holding!

These 10 titles, along with the 10 titles that preceded them, in THE TECH SET® series feature three components:

1. This book
2. Companion web content that provides more details on the topic and keeps you current
3. Author podcasts that will extend your knowledge and give you insight into the author's experience

The companion webpages and podcasts can be found at:

www.alatechsource.org/techset/

On the website, you'll go far beyond the printed pages you're holding and:

- ▶ Access author updates that are packed with new advice and recommended resources
- ▶ Use the website comments section to interact, ask questions, and share advice with the authors and your LIS peers
- ▶ Hear these pros in screencasts, podcasts, and other videos providing great instruction on getting the most out of the latest library technologies

For more information on THE TECH SET® series and the individual titles, visit **www.neal-schuman.com/techset-11-to-20**.

FOREWORD

New location-based services such as Foursquare, Brightkite, and Gowalla let people check in at venues via their mobile devices and connect with their friends in the area. Augmented reality applications let mobile users tap into a layer of information about their current location that gets displayed on top of their view of the real world. Both of these cutting-edge technologies offer a world of opportunities for libraries to enhance patrons' experience and promote the library's services. In *Location-Aware Services and QR Codes for Libraries*, mobile guru Joe Murphy provides a complete overview of the augmented reality and location-based technology landscapes and details how to use these new services in your library. This exceptional volume is jam-packed with project ideas such as how to create Foursquare, Gowalla, and QR code campaigns in your library, how to set up a location-based photostream that patrons can contribute to, how to design an augmented reality initiative, and how to implement a mobile payment service with Google Wallet for your library.

The ten new TECH SET volumes are designed to be even more cutting-edge than the original ten. After the first ten were published and we received such positive feedback from librarians who were using the books to implement technology in their libraries as well as train their staff, it seemed that there would be a need for another TECH SET. And I wanted this next set of books to be even more forward-looking and tackle today's hottest technologies, trends, and practices to help libraries stay on the forefront of technology innovation. Librarians have ceased sitting on the sidelines and have become technology leaders in their own right. This series was created to offer guidance and inspiration to all those aspiring to be library technology leaders themselves.

I originally envisioned a series of books that would offer accessible, practical information that would teach librarians not only how to use new technologies as individuals but also how to plan and implement particular types of library services using them. And when THE TECH SET won the ALA's Greenwood Publishing Group Award for the Best Book in Library Literature, it seemed that we had achieved our goal of becoming the go-to resource for libraries wanting hands-on technology primers. For these new ten books, I thought it was important to incorporate reader feedback by adding two new chapters that would better facilitate learning how to put these new technologies into practice in libraries. The new chapter called "Social Mechanics" discusses strategies for gaining buy-in and support from organizational stakeholders, and the additional "Developing Trends" chapter looks ahead to future directions of these technologies. These new chapters round out the books that discuss the entire life cycle of these tech initiatives, including everything from what it takes to plan, strategize, implement, market, and measure the success of these projects.

While each book covers the A–Zs of each technology being discussed, the hands-on "Implementation" chapters, chock-full of detailed project instructions, account for the largest portions of the books. These chapters start off with a basic "recipe" for how to effectively use the technology in a library and then build on that foundation to offer more and more advanced project ideas. Designed to appeal to readers of all levels of expertise, both the novice and advanced technologist will find something useful in these chapters, as the proposed projects and initiatives run the gamut from the basic how to create a Foursquare campaign for your library to how to build an iPhone application. Similarly, the new Drupal webmaster will benefit from the instructions for how to configure a basic library website, while the advanced web services librarian may be interested in the instructions for powering a dynamic library website in the cloud using Amazon's EC2 service.

I have been watching and learning from Joe Murphy's innovative presentations at library events for years and have determined that the popularity of his talks goes beyond his extensive knowledge of mobile trends to his ability to inspire others to get excited about new technology and to think about what's on the horizon. *Library Journal* identified him as a rising star in 2009 when they recognized him with their Movers & Shakers Award, and they were right to do so. Joe is the authority on mobile technology trends in libraries and that really shines through in his exceptional book *Location-Aware Services and QR Codes for Libraries*. Get ready to be on the cutting-edge with the hottest mobile technologies of today and tomorrow!

Ellyssa Kroski
Manager of Information Systems
New York Law Institute
http://www.ellyssakroski.com/
http://oedb.org/blogs/ilibrarian/
ellyssakroski@yahoo.com

Ellyssa Kroski is the Manager of Information Systems at the New York Law Institute as well as a writer, educator, and international conference speaker. In 2011, she won the ALA's Greenwood Publishing Group Award for the Best Book in Library Literature for THE TECH SET, the ten-book technology series that she created and edited. She's also the author of *Web 2.0 for Librarians and Information Professionals*, a well-reviewed book on web technologies and libraries. She speaks at several conferences a year, mainly about new tech trends, digital strategy, and libraries. She is an adjunct faculty member at Pratt Institute and blogs at *iLibrarian*.

PREFACE

Location-Aware Services and QR Codes for Libraries is for the librarian ready to greet the future and willing to meet a major technology trend head-on as well as converting those with higher resistance. It will directly help those working in libraries who are looking for information on location-aware technology and what this change will mean for our libraries and our jobs. *Location-Aware Services and QR Codes for Libraries* serves as a complete practical guide to this suite of technologies to help librarians become best informed by understanding the trend's implications and applications. This book's purpose is to give librarians the information they need to successfully explore and implement location-aware technologies in their own library environments.

Location-Aware Services and QR Codes for Libraries was written from the point of view of a library practitioner and geared toward fellow practitioners. It was compiled to follow my own real-world explorations and experience with these technologies as a heavy user and as a librarian exploring and implementing them in my workplace. The content was also decided upon from my experience teaching and consulting at libraries on this subject. I've had the luck of being informed as a user of these tools, bringing a human element and user perspective to the real-world side of investigating the tools.

I wrote *Location-Aware Services and QR Codes for Libraries* for two pressing reasons. The first reason is that librarians have a need for and face a struggle staying current on this important technology. There is a gap in our professional resources for gaining this knowledge that this book fills. The second reason for writing this book was that I witnessed librarians needing a fluency in this suite of technologies and their appropriate application. I have seen, after talks I have given on this topic, many librarians create a presence for their library on a location-based network for instance without considering the patron side of what it means for engagement. There is a need for an extension of technology literacy into these tools to make sure we are using them correctly, sensibly, and strategically.

► AUDIENCE AND ORGANIZATION

Location-Aware Services and QR Codes for Libraries is written for frontline staff to help them be aware of a major technology and the patron expectations it influences and for service designers so that they can successfully implement these technologies. Library school students will also find this book useful as an aid for emerging professionals becoming excellently prepared for work in our libraries who will face a tremendous growth in location-sensitive technology. It is also written to help administrators gain a thorough understanding of the options and implications of these technologies and to make informed decisions and allocations for their libraries pursuing these technology trends.

Location-Aware Services and QR Codes for Libraries is organized to bring the reader from idea to implementation with chapters and sections devoted to each major practical topic. It is laid out to bring the reader from start to finish across the steps of learning about and then implementing the technologies. There is a consistent focus on understanding the user side of the technologies and creating an awareness of the implications. Chapter 1 introduces the various location-aware applications and programs that are the driving force behind these emerging technologies. Chapter 2 explains the advantages and disadvantages of location-based services, augmented reality programs, mobile photo-sharing applications, and QR codes. Chapter 3 considers these technologies in the bigger picture for libraries and technology trends so that we can ensure that our applications of these technologies remain a relevant and viable enterprise in a changing world. Chapter 4 shows how to secure buy-in from management and get staff peers on board by creating excitement around the project. Chapter 5 delves into implementing these services. I cover how to create a Foursquare campaign and use it to enhance staff training, use Facebook Places to connect with patrons, create an augmented reality program and use it for shelf reading, create a QR code campaign, create a Gowalla marketing initiative, create a location-based photostream, and leverage social recommendation and local discovery services. I also show how to implement a mobile payment service with Google Wallet and Near Field communication. Chapter 6 offers ways to market the projects to make sure that potential users are aware of the services and their benefits and to advertise the value of the library's presence in and engagement with these technologies. Chapter 7 discusses the best practices for implementing such technology programs to ensure success for the project's long-term goals. Chapter 8 covers metrics, which help us gauge our approaches to the programs, assess our methods, and plan for future steps. Chapter 9 considers those future steps in the broader context of the developing trends.

Location-Aware Services and QR Codes for Libraries can be used as a guide to understanding and applying these technologies with information on exactly how to implement them. It can be used as a text with library and information science courses for helping library students prepare as informed service providers. It can also be used as a loose road map to exploring future technology trends as a rough outline to best practices for approaching and implementing technologies in library settings.

▶1

INTRODUCTION

- ▶ **Using Location-Aware Services and QR Codes**
- ▶ **Using These Services in the Library**
- ▶ **How This Book Will Help**

▶USING LOCATION-AWARE SERVICES AND QR CODES

One of the first things I do when I walk into my favorite restaurant is check in on Foursquare to share where I am with my network. I open the Foursquare iPhone application, browse or search for the restaurant entry, add a note about what I am doing there, and check in. I directly engage the location and/or business through its virtual representation as well as my network by checking in. I get a reward of social engagement by sharing my location and what I am doing with my contacts similar to how I am socially rewarded when I post a Tweet or Facebook status. I select the level of privacy before I complete the check-in to choose with whom I want to share my location. In this way I control my privacy and maintain the level of sharing that I have decided is appropriate for the audience of my Foursquare "followers." After checking in I look to see who else has engaged this venue, because I know that I automatically share at least one thing in common with anyone else who has checked in there—interest in this location (see Figure 1.1).

I also connect with people on Foursquare based on previous connections. People I am connected with on Facebook or Twitter are likely people I would want to share with in this other medium. I know that following professional colleagues on Foursquare can yield useful current awareness information, so I make sure to connect with them on Foursquare as well. I also will make sure to search for and follow my new and old friends as a point of staying in touch.

I may elect to check in using the newer Facebook Places location-based service if I want to share this particular activity with my established Facebook community. I open my Facebook mobile application, navigate to the Places feature, and check in, maybe with an additional text annotation (see Figure 1.2).

► Figure 1.1: Foursquare Explore View

► Figure 1.2: Facebook Places Screen

I may also ask to tag a friend along with me on my check-in or check them in myself if they've allowed it in their settings as a way of connecting us as co-sharing this activity. I have already set up my privacy settings for Facebook to share my Places check-ins with certain groups of my contacts, so I know exactly who is seeing the information and can manage my privacy at the audience level. I get the reward of connecting my activities with my contacts in Facebook Places by sharing my location with these existing social connections.

I decide to also check in on Gowalla while at this venue to interact with a partially different audience. I browse by nearby spots in the Gowalla iPhone application until I find my location based on either proximity or category (see Figure 1.3). If I am the first to check in at that location I create the spot, adding the identifying metadata that will allow other users to find and engage it as well as to earn more in game points for myself. I know that my friends on Gowalla may be more interested than my Foursquare followers in my travels, for instance, so I check in to Gowalla first at the airport. Because I have more purely professional contacts in this network, my check-ins with Gowalla tend to be more work oriented, building and strengthening my professional network while adding professional elements to my interaction with the place.

I might also open up Booyah's MyTown, a favorite location-based social network that is heavy on the gaming elements. If I have the time and check

▶ Figure 1.3: Gowalla Check-In Screen

in there as well I can increase my game rewards and expand opportunities for real-world benefits. Same for Loopt Star, InCrowd, and SCVNGR.

Location crops up in other social aspects of my everyday life. I use Gowalla to browse for restaurants by category, utilizing it as a practical discovery tool and not just as a game. I want to find a nearby restaurant with lunch discounts, so I check out what nearby places are offering deals to Foursquare users, letting location-based advertising and not just proximity help guide my selection of places to visit. I add my location to my Twitter posts through its optional location feature to tie my ideas to my locale and use Yelp to find and learn about nearby restaurants.

A new professional contact scans the QR code on my business card or presentation slide and adds my contact information directly into his mobile phone, engaging a physical platform at a specific place to access my digital data. While riding the train, I scan a QR code on a poster for a state park that I would like more information about so I can plan my trip on the go. I use this to connect to electronic information through the place-specific platform. I scan a QR code in a magazine advertisement to watch the full preview of an upcoming TV show. I use QR code–scanning mobile applications on my iPhone to access pieces of digital information contained in or linked from these small two-dimensional bar codes that here serve as a mobile bridge between digital information and physical platforms.

With augmented reality I access information about my location through my smartphone camera, using the phone's built-in GPS feature and directional tool to determine my location and pull up digital information about what I point the phone at. I scan a picture in a book with an augmented reality program to view a dynamic perspective with animation and interactive information. I scan a street scene with augmented reality mobile applications and see additional layers of information about the store fronts based on my location, including user reviews, architectural progress, and more. I can see and experience the digital information about a location that is not visible to the naked eye but that can add to my information experience with it. I scan a landscape and pull up geological information about recent earthquakes. I can see the value of a building and other real estate information just by scanning it through my smartphone augmented reality application. With augmented reality applications I am able to access visual representations of supplemental digital information that appears to fill three-dimensional space. All this with my mobile device capable of detecting my location as the portal.

In each of my described activities, I leveraged location as an aspect of social interaction through mobile technology to enhance my engagement with places, people, and data. These behaviors, these means of interaction through location-aware technologies, can be applied to library services and future directions as influencers on trends for information engagement and tools and through direct service applications.

►USING THESE SERVICES IN THE LIBRARY

Location-based social networks, QR codes, and augmented reality all leverage the power of place as a connecting point to information engagement through social or digital interaction. Location itself and the emphasis on hyperrelevance of proximity-sensitive data is a trend of concern for librarians. Location as a point to engage, a way to interact, or a platform for interaction is expanding as a technology trend across mobile and digital technologies and beginning to impact cultural expectations. Its social spread and real-world practical applications are making it a transformative technology concept. And it's spreading to libraries, with opportunities for applying location-aware technology to libraries and leveraging its influence on people's behavior and the evolution of information systems.

The stories I began with represent my real-life personal use of location-aware technologies. I try to apply the lessons learned as a user to my experiences as an information professional. I step back and look at my takeaways from these activities as a librarian, with my service provider hat on, and consider how this behavior may impact expectations for libraries as service centers. Each step and aspect of engaging these technologies has implications for demands on usage of the library as a destination and as an information portal, and we will explore exactly how to apply and how to plan for these implications.

Facebook's launch of its location engagement features represents a major breakthrough for location-based services because its status as the largest existing social network, with 800 million users, forces libraries to pay heed to this trend. My first thoughts as a user of Facebook Places for possible library applications are teaching patrons skills for controlling their privacy settings and harnessing the rich potential for connections within Facebook by applying the options for Places venues and enriching the connected venue Facebook page. We will cover exactly how to claim and manage these spaces.

When entering a library I am going to check in on Foursquare as I do at any location. However, I will not be able to fully engage the library and all it has to offer through this medium unless the library itself is taking steps to engage and support the patron experience through it. The library may not offer a promotion to those who check in the most, so my motivation to return tied to my engagement through this technology may not be as high as possible. If the library has not posted "Tips" about its location, then it misses this opportunity to increase interaction with tailored information pushed to me when checking in. The library cannot gain from the tool and its potential to reach patrons unless it actively engages it. Yes, I will still leverage the Foursquare experience as a user regardless of what the library does simply by personally using the check-in as a platform for social sharing. However, the library can literally enhance that experience for me by supporting community through it, offering incentives to engage, and using it as a platform for service. The implication for libraries as places of the widespread adoption of these tools is that our engagement with the tools can be harnessed to foster a connection with patrons and enter their daily mobile life flow. We will learn how to leverage Foursquare for these means.

These tools and their rapid expansion throughout technology also have implications for information engagement. The major ways this might be expressed are in shifting expectations for information portals, information-seeking behavior, and roles for location as connecting points to data and checking in for manipulation of information. As a heavy user of Foursquare I get used to its browsing and searching functions in my everyday life, causing me to begin expecting similar discovery features in library tools and other information resources. In this way, my usage of Foursquare is influencing my expectations for using library resources. I also begin to wish that my ability to use location to find related venues and people can be translated into information discovery methods based on local relevance. Foursquare is becoming a habitual technology whose usage is shaping expectations. Other technologies, most notably QR codes and augmented reality, are not important to libraries yet as critical mass tools but rather as tools with immense potential for libraries acting to meet a changing data sphere.

▶ HOW THIS BOOK WILL HELP

I introduce the tools of location-based services, QR codes, and augmented reality, providing a basic survey of the landscape of each technology type and its real-world human and practical uses. I explore the implications of the location-sensitive tools for information engagement and thus for libraries.

Librarians must understand the tools and the worldview they function in as well as the trends they are guiding in order to understand the implications for their libraries. To accomplish this, I will walk through the specifics of the technologies and each major resource within them, their functions and features, and their uses and benefits, everything that we need to know in order to understand the culture and expectations they thrive in and that they create as well as the opportunities for libraries. We will also explore the unique details of each technology so that we can make informed decisions as librarians looking to implement these tools to enhance library services and as service providers hoping to understand their impacts on changing expectations for information engagement.

The hardest part of implementing new technology is often overcoming the fear of that new technology. Tips for advocacy, tricks for gaining buy-in, and advice for tweaking the internal marketing steps for each of our own unique library environments will be a key first step.

We will build upon the knowledge that we gain about each of these technologies to cover possible uses of them in library settings. We will start with the direct implementations of tools that are easily applicable for most libraries, including how to use Foursquare for marketing the library and driving foot traffic, what type of presence to have on Gowalla, how to create QR codes for improving access, how to design and evaluate the impact of augmented reality pilots, and how to connect with patrons within and with the help of each. We will go through every step and stage so that together we are fully fluent in exactly how to implement these technologies in our libraries.

Then we will talk about applications that take a bit of creativity and flexibility for enhancing existing library services and operations with these technologies. We will explore going beyond the basics and into advanced applications that twist the technologies and the concepts to not just the current needs of our libraries but also the future directions of this trend.

Although marketing is tricky, it is key to the success of location-aware technology programs. Advertising library usage of these emerging tools must tackle both staff and user education while balancing added value to library services. Our understanding of these tools can inform marketing strategies that leverage their benefits and their intrigue. Some of these technologies are alien to end users, and marketing their value may begin with exposing their existence, introducing their uses, and then inserting their benefits to patrons.

After the practical how-to details of implementation comes the realistic side of what challenges we will encounter and how to overcome them. We ask what new approaches to staffing and management these tools require. We will connect library staff work flows with procedures that are part and parcel with using these tools. There is only so far that new technologies will bend toward working in our existing models. So, reshaping how we do things—how we staff, monitor, and evaluate services with these tools— requires new ways of doing the work of libraries, including structures for creating and responding in these new venues, reallocating staff time to virtual platforms, and dedicating time to creating and revising QR code images and augmented reality data resources.

There are real-world management considerations and new staff skills that these technologies force libraries to address. A library connecting with patrons on Foursquare, for instance, must deal with the private and sensitive data of patrons that it will have access to. By using Foursquare to measure library traffic statistics, libraries have access to patron information that has an expectation of privacy, so we have to assign policies for staff engaging the technology that safeguards that data. We will also need to provide the staff time for implementing and measuring services using QR codes that complement, not ignore or swamp, the traditional work and services that already fill their time and realign resources so that we can investigate augmented reality applications.

Location-aware technologies, including location-based services, QR codes, and augmented reality, are moving beyond being a trend to becoming a focus of technology advancement that is changing how we engage with information, places, and each other. The ways that librarians and patrons conceive and use physical library spaces are changing along with the advancements in location-aware technology. Traditional venues for library services, including information discovery, collections, reference, and more, will continue to change under these pressures. The possible and likely changing roles of the public, academic, and school libraries in this evolving future will be directly impacted by these technological and cultural changes, and libraries considering these changes now can adapt to the further pressures to come. The new face of library services in a location-aware world is a rich arena with opportunities for librarians learning about the tools now. There certainly is a place for the library in the emerging location-focused technological world, but we librarians have to work to insert the library into this shifting paradigm.

The future directions and developing trends with these technologies are as important for librarians to consider as is the current state. We can expect the developing trends to include the further permeation of location as a relevancy point and its role as a platform for interaction to continue its expansion. We can expect the role of location in discovery and social collaboration based on proximity to grow. Awareness and spread of informational applications of QR codes will swell as they enter the realm of cultural literacy, and augmented reality will transition smoothly into a common information resource as smartphones proliferate. These trends and directions will impact libraries whether or not we meet them head-on. But, as informed professionals aware of their impact and fluent in their applications, we librarians can guide the development of our libraries to best move in tandem with these trends, benefit from them, and assist our end users in using them effectively.

▶2

TYPES OF SOLUTIONS AVAILABLE

▶ **Recognize the Emerging Implications of Location for Library Services**

▶ **Consider the Major Technologies of Location-Aware Services**

▶ **Consider the Most Popular Applications**

Location-aware technologies are becoming a popular part of the information and social experiences within our daily life flows. They are helping to transform the concept of where we are into a point of interactivity.

▶RECOGNIZE THE EMERGING IMPLICATIONS OF LOCATION FOR LIBRARY SERVICES

The use of location-based services within our lives as well as their roles with our experiences with information continue to expand. Location-based services such as Foursquare are used for sharing your location and activities with your social connections. By checking in at a location with Foursquare, you are telling your friends who also use the service where you are and are sharing your activities associated with that location. Foursquare, Gowalla, and Facebook Places are also used for building social connections based on that shared location.

The expansion of these technologies is altering the roles of location in our social and information experiences. These location-based services are beginning to impact the expectations our patrons have for libraries because of their heavy use in other areas of their lives. Some of those impacted expectations as well as a few of the larger implications for information services and spaces include the following:

> ▶ How we expect to engage with a place we visit is changing. Consider the ways we are now used to interacting with the virtual representation of the building through our mobile devices.

► How we discover information is also changing. Using a browsable list ranked by proximity and imput from our local peers is increasingly common, which impacts electronic library content.

► The prioritization of checking into visited locations may mean that social behaviors within that location are affected, with a new focus on checking in with the mobile device as primary behavior before in-person greetings.

► Checking in as part of our established behaviors within a place means that patrons may deem it acceptable to multitask: interacting with service staff while checking in on their smartphone.

► Visitors may be checking in before using the functions of the space, changing the flow of foot traffic. New areas of congregation may crop up where people want to stop for a moment to check in.

► People checking in have a new need for knowing the exact name of the location so that they know what venue to check in at within location-based services. This impacts locations such as libraries because we want patrons to check in to the correct venue so that the statistic goes to our library. So, there is now a need for clear visual cues to the name of the library venue within the library itself.

► Physical browsing may become part of a series of engagements with locations or a trail with micro rewards at each spot.

► Just as searching with Google has changed the way we expect to search online, searching within Foursquare may impact how we expect to search for or by location.

► Location-based services compel us to search for nearby deals, fostering a reward system based on proximity as a relevancy point.

► Checking in is becoming a level of engagement with a place, and locations can leverage that activity as an opportunity to interact and improve patron experience.

► Users may be developing expectations for in-game rewards for engaging. When we check in we expect to earn badges, stickers, mayorships, and points.

► There is also a growing expectation that in-game accomplishments should lead to rewards in real life. At minimum, this should include acknowledgment of mayorships won.

► Some points of discovery are increasingly based on service reviews within location-based services such as Foursquare Tips.

► Being able to add to the visual narrative of a location is becoming an expectation. Users enjoy adding photos to Foursquare venues, checking in with Gowalla, tagging pages in Facebook, and contributing to Instagram. So, policies against taking photos within our libraries may be perceived as limits to our established behaviors.

▶ CONSIDER THE MAJOR TECHNOLOGIES OF LOCATION-AWARE SERVICES

This section provides a general overview of the technology landscape and the major areas of location-aware social technologies for libraries.

Location-Based Services

Location-based services are exciting mobile applications that make a game out of visiting real-world places. They make visiting your favorite places even more fun by providing in-app rewards among your peers for playing the game and, even better, rewards in the real world by claiming prizes offered by the locations themselves through the apps. These game-like mobile services make it rewarding to visit and check in to your nearby places because they offer practical benefits like discounts and a social way to discover new places to check out in your neighborhood. Major applications include Foursquare, Gowalla, and Facebook Places. Use Foursquare to reward people for visiting your library, Facebook Places to drive traffic of specified groups to the library, and Gowalla to advertise your library's physical location with this digital community. Location-based applications hold power and promise for your library because they serve as a popular new form of local discovery that can include your library, they allow the library to enter into the reward structure of choosing where to go, and they help keep the library in view of and a part of the local scene.

Augmented Reality

Imagine looking at a building through your smartphone and seeing how it used to look or scanning a store front and having displays of user reviews pop up. Augmented reality technologies display layers of digital information over the view of real-world objects and places through the lens of mobile applications. These applications augment your view of reality by displaying the rich online data associated with objects and places. Mobile augmented reality applications use your mobile device's three features of its camera, location as determined by its GPS chip, and accelerometer or similar device that determines the direction it is pointing. These combine to determine what information is associated with the objects or places in the device's view. It then displays that added information on top of the virtual display.

Augmented reality applications can be used to provide library resources in your community, allowing patrons to add their own tidbits of digital information to the library's surfaces and mobilizing staff work flows such as shelf reading. I find that these examples of augmented reality help to illuminate the technology:

▶ The Layar application pulls information from data layers selected by the user to display everything from Yelp reviews and Foursquare check-ins to *Wikipedia* entries about places in view.

▶ The Pocket Universe application shows you information about astronomical objects that are within your virtual view as you point your iPad at the sky day or night.

Mobile Photo-Sharing Applications

Mobile photo-sharing applications, including Instagram, picplz, and Path, are location-sensitive networks that allow users to snap photos, manipulate images with filters, post to a community, add as a visual element to a location, and share with their social networks or with nearby users.

QR Codes

Imagine being able to scan something with your smartphone and immediately be linked to online information about that object or place. This is the power of QR codes, small bar codes, often about the size of a postage stamp, that contain links or customized information revealed when scanned with a smartphone. QR codes are created with free online generators, are usually used in picture formats, and can contain far more information than traditional bar codes. QR codes can contain links, open text, contact information, calendar event files, app downloads, videos, and more. QR codes on real estate signs can contain links to information about the property. QR codes on business windows can include hours. QR codes in magazine articles can link to the resources being discussed.

▶ CONSIDER THE MOST POPULAR APPLICATIONS

This section covers the major options, products, and concepts of location-aware technology in the context of service providers.

Location-Based Services

Some of the growing suite of tools that gamify social location check-ins include the following:

▶ **Foursquare:** This is the dominant location-based social network that allows users to check in to their location in a game-like mobile application. Foursquare rewards users for checking in at locations with points, a chance to compete for the title of mayor at their favorite venues, and earn rewards from participating businesses/libraries.

- **Facebook Places:** A location check-in service within Facebook, Places allows users to share their location and activity with their friends in this large existing social network and adds a location element to the sharing stream.
- **Gowalla:** Gowalla is a more personalized location-based social network competing with but also growing alongside Foursquare. Gowalla offers more levels of rewards, including pins, stamps, items, and leaderboard points, as well as greater user personalization with custom trips and highlights. Gowalla is less about competition and more about achieving individual rewards, including custom stamps from featured locations and special items associated with real-world current events.

See the companion website at http://www.alatechsource.org/techset/ for more details on this topic.

QR Codes

QR codes are bar codes that can be scanned with smartphones using the device's camera and a mobile application. QR codes contain more information than bar codes and that information can include anything from links to open text.

QR Code Generators

To create QR codes, you can use any one of several free QR code generators that you can find in a Google search for the phrase "QR code generators." Here are a few of the diverse generators that will be useful for your library and some information about their features to help you decide which to use:

- http://qrcode.kaywa.com is a very basic and very easy-to-use generator that offers four types of content for QR codes: link as URL web address, text for just open readable text-based content, a phone number that can be stored or called from a scanned code, or SMS that can be used to populate a text message with preprogrammed content to a designated cell phone number. Once your content has been inputted, you can choose the size of code to generate, save the code as an image, or grab the provided HTML code to embed it.
- http://zxing.appspot.com/generator/ offers several more content options, including calendar event with full details, full contact information, e-mail address, geolocation, phone number, SMS, text, URL, and Wi-Fi network to share SSID and passwords via a scan.
- http://www.qrstuff.com/ allows you to create codes with text, URL, telephone number, SMS message, e-mail address, e-mail message, contact

details in vCard format, events as vCalendar, Google Maps location, Wi-Fi Login for Android only, PayPal Buy Now links, social media profiles links, iTunes links, and YouTube video links. The social media options it offers include Twitter profile usernames, Twitter status updates, Facebook profile links, Facebook Like links, MySpace profile links, LinkedIn profiles, LinkedIn Share, and Foursquare venues.

► http://delivr.com/qr-code-generator offers basic options, including URL, contact information, e-mail address, phone number, SMS, and open text, as well as a unique set of options including SMS to short codes, links to popular social media services with the root URLs already attached, mobile application store links for the Android and Apple marketplaces, Yelp venues, and Foursquare locations.

► http://goqr.me/ offers the same basic options as the generators already mentioned—text, URL, phone, SMS, and vCard contact information—but it also offers the unique feature to change the color of the code's pixels and its background to create a QR code that will really stand out.

► Another easy way to create QR codes with links is through one of the several major URL shortening services. Bitly and Google's Goo.gl have both added features for creating QR codes from their shortened web addresses. Use Bitly to create a QR code from a shortened link that can also be tracked by clicking "info plus" for the link within your Bitly account. Or simply add ".qr" at the end of any link you have shortened with Google's http://goo.gl/ to generate a QR code for that shortened link.

QR Code Readers

QR code scanning and reading applications read and translate the code to display and make the encoded information accessible. Popular QR code reader applications vary in features and cost. Try out the following recommended applications:

► QuickMark
► BeeTagg
► QR Droid
► i-nigma
► NeoReader

Augmented Reality Applications

These are some of the more popular augmented reality applications:

► **Layar:** This service provides custom data layers that you can choose from when scanning a view in order to select exactly what hidden layers of data about a location you want to display. Imagine being able to look at a scene and reveal the views of that place hidden by time or digital filter. These layers can include everything from Foursquare check-ins to architectural history. You can even create and share your own layers.

▶ **Virtual Graffiti:** This application allows you to add graffiti-like art to the walls of any building, inside or out, that you can display through the augmented reality app.

▶ **Pocket Universe:** This is a sky/star-watching application that shows you what astronomical objects are in "view" wherever you point your device, day or night.

▶ **Shelvar:** This shelf-reading application was developed to identify books shelved out of order, providing a workplace efficiency function for augmented reality tools.

Mobile Photo-Sharing Applications

Explore these popular mobile photo-sharing applications (see Figure 2.1):

▶ **Instagram:** The leading mobile photo-sharing application, Instagram lets you snap, add filters to, and share pictures taken on your smartphone. Instagram allows you to associate images with topics through hashtags and with locations, including Foursquare places. Instagram allows users to contribute to the visual narrative of a location. This application has grown at an incredibly fast rate and is regularly adding new brand partnerships.

▶ **Picplz:** Picplz functions similar to Twitter for pictures, displaying photos from those you follow in a stream. Picplz has a stronger web presence than Instagram.

▶ **Color:** This application's focus is more on location than topic or user. Photos added to Color are associated with the location at which they are taken and are available only to nearby users. Color creates a hyper local experience for adding to the visual narrative of a place and permits social discovery of other nearby users.

▶ Figure 2.1: Mobile Application Instagram, Images Taken at a Location

Other Tools

There are many other popular tools with location attributes:

- ► Yelp is a local user review service.
- ► Twitter allows optional addition of location metadata to tweets.
- ► Bizzy is a social recommendation engine that provides nearby suggestions based on input from you and your friends.
- ► Google's location products are Latitude and Google Places.
- ► Other location-based services, including Loopt, Brightkite, Whrrl, SCVNGR (see Figure 2.2), InCrowd, Neer, and Booyah's MyTown (see Figure 2.3), are making some waves but are not yet as big as Foursquare.
- ► Group messaging applications are growing rapidly and adding locally relevant discussions plus location elements to our mobile conversations. The major group messaging applications with location features include GroupMe, Yobongo, textPlus, and Beluga (see Figure 2.4).

Final Considerations

Designing implementations of location-based services starts with a thorough understanding of the technologies, their features, and unique considerations

► Figure 2.2: SCVNGR Main Page

▶Figure 2.3: MyTown Main Page

for their application. Each location-based service has its own features, brings its own strengths, and has its own set of applications for libraries. Service professionals need to make sure that they have all the information about these products as they consider applying this trend. This can include knowing what is required to use the service (e.g., Foursquare requires a download of the mobile application and an account to check in).

Criteria for evaluating the technology options include popularity of the service, penetration of individual services into your end-user groups, ability of the service to grow and adapt with changes in technology trends, applicability of the service's features to established and potential library services, and the levels of possible patron engagement it provides.

▶Figure 2.4: Icons for Major Group Messaging Mobile Applications—Beluga, textPlus, GroupMe, and Yobongo (from 2011)

▶3

PLANNING

- ▶ Consider the Big Picture
- ▶ Engage Patrons through Location-Based Themes and Trends
- ▶ Plan a Practical Strategy for Using Location-Aware Technologies in Libraries

▶CONSIDER THE BIG PICTURE

An important aspect of pursuing location-aware technologies is understanding their roles in the big picture of libraries and of technology trends. It is important to watch the big picture so that you ensure your applications of these technologies remain a relevant and viable enterprise in a changing world.

Gauging the big picture of technology trends in this area can be tricky. The best approach is to keep an eye, and your fingers, on multiple tools within the space. Keep an eye on larger trends that may impact the look of features and uses of location-aware technologies.

The big picture for their role in libraries is a bit more static. Libraries will, for the foreseeable future, have a role in physical spaces. As long as there is a location element to information services and collections, there will be a role for location-aware technology in libraries. In fact, there will always be roles for location-aware technologies, even if the only remaining information points are those tied to real-world objects and places without the presence of physical libraries.

The role of these technologies in the big picture for libraries and technology is that they give people a location-contextual experience to information. Location as access point via mobile/social technologies will remain whether it is for discovery or social interaction around content.

► ENGAGE PATRONS THROUGH LOCATION-BASED THEMES AND TRENDS

The major themes and trends for location-aware technologies as avenues of service opportunities are engaging the concepts of checking in, enhancing the patron's experience with the library's virtual representation, interacting over visual elements associated with a location, and leveraging the technologies as discovery tools.

The idea of checking in to places, events, foods, books, and television shows is a common current theme for engagement via mobile devices. Foursquare made famous the concept of location check-in, GetGlue and Miso allow entertainment check-ins, Foodspotting allows food item check-ins, and SoundTracking allows for checking into a song. The idea behind the check-in is that you are making a connection with a real-world place by signaling your interaction with its virtual representation. It is also an equivalent to the textual check-in when you announce where you are with Twitter or Facebook status updates. The location check-in is the point of interaction, marketing, and experiential engagement between a user and the location through the location-aware technology.

Using location-aware tools as social discovery resources is another growing trend. Bizzy uses your input and that of your social connections to recommend nearby venues for you. Foodspotting lets you browse pictures of food provided by close restaurants to help you decide where to go and what to eat. Foursquare recently added its Explore tab that helps you find nearby venues by category and based on your interest. Facebook Deals and Foursquare help you discover places near to you that are offering promotions, and Groupon helps you leverage group purchasing within your area.

Another major trend in location-aware technology is the addition of images as a visual element to the experience with the location. Gowalla and SCVNGR first allowed for posting pictures at venues. Foursquare then added the feature of posting pictures to check-ins and at location pages a bit later and blew by Gowalla in the number of pictures posted. Mobile photo-sharing applications such as Instagram, picplz, and Path each include a location element, and some are based around the concept of sharing images associated with a location. Instagram added a feature to let you check in to a Foursquare location when posting pictures at that location. So, adding pictures as a visual element to the local experience is a major trend.

Many venues are using location-aware technology to provide enhanced experiences for patrons with the place's virtual representation with Foursquare Tips and reviews on Yelp and Google Places. Micro deals are an emerging trend, providing brief or limited promotions to capture the interest of potential customers.

▶ PLAN A PRACTICAL STRATEGY FOR USING LOCATION-AWARE TECHNOLOGIES IN LIBRARIES

A key element is to plan a practical strategy for designing and implementing applications of location-aware technology in your library. Designing and implementing should be planned from the very beginning, and the plan should guide everything from exploration to adoption through evaluation. Practical strategies should always be informed by personal usage of the technology, not primarily from the perspective of a librarian or service provider. I recommend that you first explore the technology, then play with it in the context of your life, and then consider its library applications before thinking about the technology as a service provider. This will ensure that the ways you implement the tool will be in line with real-world expectations of that technology and that the applications of it will closely align with your patrons' expectations if they are already users.

Here is the beginning of a sample strategy for introducing Foursquare at your library:

- ▶ Download the mobile application for the service.
- ▶ Create an account.
- ▶ Think about and set your privacy preferences.
- ▶ Build a network within Foursquare of those you would like to connect and share with.
- ▶ Start checking into Foursquare at locations you visit in your real life.
- ▶ Make sure to visit libraries and a wide range of other venue types.
- ▶ Try out all aspects of the tool: checking in, sharing beyond Foursquare, following and accepting followers, exploring for places to visit, claiming specials, creating spots, uploading pictures, adding comments to check-ins, leaving tips, browsing tips, and adding To Dos.
- ▶ Consider how, as a Foursquare user, you would like to see it implemented at venues you visit.
- ▶ After using it for a little while, begin thinking about how use of it impacts your expectations upon locations you visit.
- ▶ Reflect upon how it impacts your interaction with a place and with people at that place.

As you gain experience, continue to reflect on it to gain an understanding of how your behavior has been affected. Then think about the library setting. Consider how you would envision the perfect experience with Foursquare at a library you might visit to be. Then use that vision to guide your practical strategy for using Foursquare at your library.

Practical strategies for planning applications of location-aware technologies in libraries should include the following elements:

► The perspective of a user of the location-aware technologies in planning and implementation stages
► The perspective of a user of mobile devices so that designed services are in line with expectations of your mobile patrons
► The perspective of a user of social media so that the norms and level of comfort with sharing are in tune with those of your social media–savvy patrons
► A plan for scaling up in the event of success
► A plan for scaling out to share the program with affiliated and parent bodies
► A sustainability plan to keep the service going
► A continuity plan to account for possible staff changes
► Training for all staff, project lead persons, frontline staff, interns, technical support, administrators, and marketers
► A plan for adopting the service to new platforms that may emerge for the technology
► A plan for adapting to changes in the tool itself, such as:
  ► Changes in the tool's features
  ► Changes in the tool's functions
  ► Changes to the tool's uses as it adapts
  ► Changes in the tool's appearance
► Plan for integrating the technology into tools that can be predicted to or may be expected to emerge or gain in popularity
► Plans for using the technology to enhance services not impacted in the first iteration (i.e., have primary and secondary projects ready)
► Plan to use the technology in conjunction with services that have not yet emerged (be flexible enough to adapt to as yet unknown library services)
► Plan for integrating the technology into collections for discovery and access
► An exit strategy in the event that the project is cancelled

A practical strategy including the listed elements should flow from a staff member's vision to an action plan and guiding principles/goals into actionable outcomes. Here is a more detailed sample outline for a practical strategy. If creating a Foursquare campaign at your library, it may look like this:

▶ Give lead staff an opportunity to gain experience with Foursquare. Have them download it and play with it at work and beyond.

▶ Explore current applications of Foursquare that can serve as examples to help brainstorm library applications.

▶ Investigate the probable future directions of Foursquare's development.

▶ Gain an understanding for how the behavior of future patrons may be impacted by the spread of Foursquare. Think about what it will mean for how patrons will expect to interact with the library as a place and if it will impact how they expect to discover information.

▶ Design and plan for the library's adoption of the technology.

▶ Identify the service points that can be enhanced by the technology and how those services may be impacted.

▶ Design a plan for selling the program to administration and staff and securing the buy-in necessary to begin and sustain the project.

▶ Draft staff training programs.

▶ Plan for a slow and careful rollout and testing period of the projects.

▶ Create and seek feedback on a marketing plan.

▶ Secure the needed partnerships with Foursquare representatives and community groups.

▶ Create reward systems to encourage patrons to engage your Foursquare presence.

▶ Finalize work flows for creating and staffing the various elements of a Foursquare campaign. Make sure staff know what they are supposed to do and how to do it.

▶ Create evaluation methods and make sure they are in place before beginning the program.

▶ Develop a plan for reacting with flexibility to changes with Foursquare or people's behaviors with it, and design supplemental or alternative applications of it for your library.

▶ Make sure the strategy accounts for who will maintain the library's presence in Foursquare, who will run the marketing, and who will interact with patrons.

▶4

SOCIAL MECHANICS

- ▶ Secure Buy-In from Management
- ▶ Get Staff on Board
- ▶ Create Excitement around the Project

The success of your projects that leverage location-aware tools will be affected by your ability to strategically manage the social mechanics of introducing a new technology into your institution. It is critical that you gain buy-in from peers and administration in order to successfully launch new programs. Your bosses need to be on board so that you are given the necessary time, money, and administrative support to accomplish your goals. Your fellow staff members need to be with you in supporting the projects, because they are a critical part in project execution, marketing, and sustainability.

▶SECURE BUY-IN FROM MANAGEMENT

Selling to management is not always easy. Here are some tips for approaching this important group of stakeholders. When opening the conversation, get to the point quickly to demonstrate that you are an articulate lead on this project. Project leaders need to be able to sell the idea by articulating its strengths and implications. Show your boss that you are ready for this; at the same time, you are demonstrating that you are knowledgeable about the topic.

Focus your opening pitch on how the project fits into and enhances established goals of the library. Explain how it will improve existing services and functions. Clearly articulate your reasons for pursuing the project and the positive ways it will impact the library and the community it serves. Focus on tying the goals of the project to the established strategic goals of your library. Articulate how using this technology meets those goals in a changing environment instead of focusing on adding the technology as an additional element.

Explain how you plan to implement the project. Be familiar with the steps it will take and who will complete them. Be ready with a plan for evaluating the project, and have a marketing model and a model for scaling the project up and down.

Be prepared to explain what the possible complications are of the project. Know and be honest about sharing the negative impacts of the projects. Explain the potential shortcomings, the tough spots of the plan, and the unknowns. Have a plan for addressing each of the known complications and a method for flexibly dealing with the unknown complications that will arise. Articulate how it will impact who and how those affected staff will be prepared and supported.

Address how implementing these technologies may impact staff, work flows, and job responsibilities. Explain how staff time may be affected and what the solutions are to balancing staff resources. Suggest areas of staff work that can be made simpler by these technologies as well as possible reductions in ongoing duties as you add more duties with these new technologies. Also on the matter of planning for resource investments, emphasize the concept that utilizing location-aware technologies can be a less costly approach to engaging mobile patrons than some alternative paths.

Maintain the focus of your pitch on the short-term and long-term benefits of the project. Explain the carefully thought out plan, how troubles will be addressed, and how your time and the library's resources spent on this will uncover immediate and future benefits. Mention intangible benefits, including flexible preparation for potential unfolding models of information engagement that come from patron use of the technology, but focus on benefits that fit into your institution's current value system. Mention how employing these technologies will also serve as advocacy for the library's ability to remain current and visible on top of its value toward meeting your patrons' shifting expectations for discovery.

► GET STAFF ON BOARD

Selling to staff can often be trickier. Staff tend to have a different priority system that needs to be respected and addressed in order to win them over as supporters. The focus when selling to your colleagues should be on how the project and technology will not make their work harder and how they will be supported throughout its adaptation.

Provide great detail when you introduce the concept and technology to staff, easing them into becoming familiar with the tool and its role. Then outline the goals of the project, focusing on what the benefits will be, how you as lead person will assume the responsibilities, and how you are all in it together. Then introduce how the project will unfold, what it will look like, and how they will contribute. Address the changes this will mean for their work and how they will be supported through gaining familiarity with the tool as well as the skills they will need for contributing to the project.

Leverage one of the major driving reasons to pursue location-aware technology for your library—that the physical library will continue to play an important role, that that role must continue to be supported and advocated for, and that location technologies can strongly help to meet this goal. This is a primary motivation behind its local implementation and a primary need for staff participation.

Change is always hard. So be prepared to show how you will support the emotional and mental costs of pursuing the change. Learning the new technology will be difficult for some staff, so show how you will ease that concern for them. Turn the conversation about change tensions into one of opportunities. Show how this will be an opportunity for team building.

Many of the location-aware technologies may bring with them specific concerns and stigma. Foursquare or Facebook Places may elicit concerns for protecting privacy. Have plans for work flows that address these concerns, as well as methods for immediately and openly discussing the concerns. Include in staff training activities for understanding and mastering the actual privacy issues and dispel myths. Have a plan for helping all staff and bosses enter the world of the technology usage so they can understand projects from the view of technology users.

A common barrier to getting staff on board with technology projects is how intimidating these new tools can seem. You can counter this barrier by employing tactics that focus on and minimize that emotional reaction, including using an iPad instead of an iPhone for demonstrations because its screen is larger and less intimidating. Use story examples that include demographics besides the young to show that the technology is approachable by their peers.

▶ CREATE EXCITEMENT AROUND THE PROJECT

You are functioning as an advocate now, as a salesperson for the future. Remember that people don't like to be sold to. The project can benefit from staff and administration feeling as though the idea is in line with their own thoughts and values. Help them arrive at the same conclusion about the interest and importance of the project. Sell the excitement around the idea, and be there to help envision a way to get there. Here are some tips:

► Place the benefits of the location-aware technology within the narrative of the library's current and future priorities.

► Focus your conversations about the potential project on the capital of attention for marketing and public relations for the library's modernity that this idea will generate.

► Start conversations about it with your direct boss. Respect proper channels, and prepare your supervisor for bringing the idea up further as needed.

► Demonstrate that you have done your homework. Mention other libraries or organizations that have tried it, and be prepared to reveal any data on the technology and related services.

► Align your selling points very closely, transparently, and within the published strategic goals of your library. Show how they can serve as actionable outcomes toward those goals.

► Speak to the traditional strengths of the library.

► Focus on application strengths that will grow with established areas of interest.

► Discuss the technologies as mainstream when possible, not outliers or new fads or trends, to show that this is worth pursuing and their energy won't be wasted.

► Mention the coming changes as easy transitions that the institution is prepared to address.

► Gain allies first. Find and secure your supporters among your peers before making official pushes.

► Create local champions who will go forward and sell for you. Find those who share an interest or are likely to feel excitement about the technology and its applications. Work with them to show others the tool's benefit independently before selling it as a service so that staff members have an idea of its value as people before they analyze it as a service.

▶5

IMPLEMENTATION

- ▶ Create a Foursquare Campaign for Your Library
- ▶ Use Foursquare to Support Staff Work
- ▶ Use Facebook Places to Connect with Patrons
- ▶ Create an Augmented Reality Program in Your Library
- ▶ Create a Library QR Code Campaign
- ▶ Create a Gowalla Marketing Initiative for Your Library
- ▶ Create a Location-Based Photo Stream for Your Library
- ▶ Leverage Social Recommendation and Local Discovery Services
- ▶ Implement a Mobile Payment Service with Google Wallet and Near Field Communication at Your Library

Now that we have introduced the various types of solutions available and explored how to make sure everyone is on board with the projects, let's talk about how to implement these technologies at our libraries.

▶CREATE A FOURSQUARE CAMPAIGN FOR YOUR LIBRARY

Foursquare is a location-based social network with many exciting opportunities for libraries. With Foursquare, patrons can check in to your library location, share their activity with their social networks, and benefit from added value that you may append to your library's virtual presence within the network. Here are the activities we'll be discussing in this project:

- ▶ Creating a new account
- ▶ Claiming your venue
- ▶ Confirming your venue
- ▶ Using specials and prizes
- ▶ Giving rewards for mayorships
- ▶ Giving other rewards
- ▶ Adding tips
- ▶ Creating a badge
- ▶ Tracking performance

Creating a New Account

The first step is to create a new Foursquare account so that you can start to leverage all that Foursquare has to offer your library. Before you can begin offering exciting rewards and specials to your patrons, you must first establish an account and claim your library's venue. Here's how.

You have a couple of choices with regard to your account; you can either set up a new account for employees to share independent of any one staff member or you can have staff members use their own existing independent account with which to interact with your library's Foursquare presence. When weighing these options, make sure to consider privacy for staff and staff accounts, the appearance of the account and the message it presents, the name of the interacting account, proper interaction conventions for guiding behavior, e-mail alerts to be aware of activity and respond in a timely manner, and other impacted work flows.

Using the method of setting up an account for staff to share independent of other staff members may be better for sustainability and continuity than allowing staff to use their existing accounts, but it depends on and is subject to more complicated management and training considerations. Because it is not one person's account in particular, accountability must be assigned to ensure the account is engaged properly and thoroughly. Such an account can be created from the Foursquare home screen when signed out or from within the claiming venue process when it offers the opportunity to choose.

There are quite a few considerations and best practices to keep in mind if you decide to create a new account for staff to use for managing your library's Foursquare presence as opposed to having them utilize their own established accounts. These include associating your account with an established Facebook account and carefully choosing a username, user icon, real name, e-mail address, location, and phone number. You can easily create and log in to a Foursquare account with an existing Facebook account, but do this only if there already exists an account in Facebook for your library like the one you want to create in Foursquare; in other words, use only a similar staff Facebook account to create a staff Foursquare account.

The username for your library staff's account should be consistent with your other social media accounts and should be as short as possible while being recognizable and findable. The icon photo should not be left to the default but rather should be chosen to represent the library or its staff in as simple and clear a way as possible. The picture will be publicly viewable to all. The real name of the account should definitely be used so that it makes clear that the account is not spam, demonstrates its identity, and assists with findability. The e-mail address chosen to be associated with the account should fill several functions: be accessible to all involved staff or the point person, be an address at which patrons can reliably and regularly reach staff, and appear official and obviously associated with the library staff.

The given location of the account should be that of the library in the same terms that a patron would think to name it. A gender must be selected, but this data does not affect the service. A birth date must also be chosen to "provide only age-appropriate access to content." The phone number is not required, but I highly suggest including it so that you maximize how reachable your library's staff are within this network. The phone number also deserves consideration to plan ahead for the possibility that the account will be associated with a mobile phone.

Claiming Your Venue

Next you will want to claim your library's Foursquare venue. As a Foursquare user, you can "claim" the library's venue online by clicking on the "Do you manage this venue? Claim here" tab on the venue's site as long as it has not already been claimed (see Figure 5.1).

Foursquare's Venue

In Foursquare, the site set aside for each location is known as a "venue." A location's venue is the virtual representation of that place where a user checks in. Venue pages include such information as address, who else is checked in, mayor information, details on specials, tips about that location left by users, and the Foursquare Lists added by users.

You will have to go through several steps to prove that you do in fact have the authority to claim control over your library's venue. Once you have clicked to claim the venue, you will have to agree to terms of use and verify

▶ Figure 5.1: Claim Your Foursquare Venue

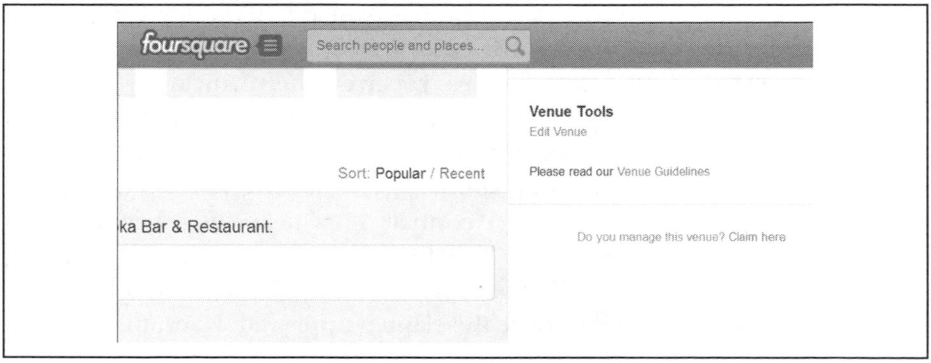

that you are in fact authorized. Read the "Authorized Venue Platform Terms of Use" at http://foursquare.com/legal/venueterms, and click "Yes, I am authorized, and I agree to the Venue Platform Terms of Use." Next, confirm that you want to publicly link the library venue to your Foursquare account. The account you are currently signed into will be linked to your library's public venue, so this is an important management step with implications for staff. Considerations for library staff at this stage include the privacy of the associated Foursquare user and the staffing work flow. For the library, make sure that the account holder claiming the venue (1) is the correct and agreed upon person to manage your Foursquare presence (don't have someone just randomly claim it without thinking this through) and (2) has been included in a continuity plan in the event that he or she leaves your library in the future; your ability to leverage Foursquare should not be contingent on any one staff member. It is important here that you choose the correct account and consider the operational impacts of using this particular account.

Confirming Your Claim

Whether you are claiming a venue with a newly created account or with an existing staff member's account, Foursquare will next ask you to identify if the venue location for your library is a chain or one of a kind. Usually library branches are distinct enough to warrant being identified as not a chain.

There are currently two confirmation methods for authorizing your account's access to your library's venue: entering a phone number that matches directory listings or a mailing address to which a verification code can be sent. Confirming via the library's phone number is a simple process that involves verifying that the number already associated with the account matches that listed in the national phone directories that Foursquare uses.

Alternatively, you can verify through the mail. If the mailing address listed for the venue is correct, select this method to have Foursquare mail you an envelope containing a verification code and a Foursquare window cling sticker along with detailed instructions for completing the claiming verification process (see Figure 5.2). After you have received the verification code and entered it into Foursquare, you will receive a message via e-mail only that explains the next steps for proceeding with the venue claim (see Figure 5.3).

Claims submitted for managing venues are first reviewed by Foursquare employees to ensure honesty in venue control. This means that there can be a delay in processing claim requests. I have heard rumors of some claims taking as long as several months to verify. So, plan ahead for this possibility. Claim your library early, and be ready to act once the claim is approved. Insert the claiming step into the early preliminary actions for your library's Foursquare strategy.

▶ Figure 5.2: Confirm Your Venue by Postal Mail

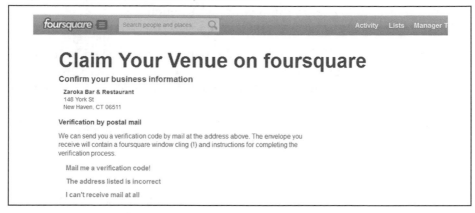

Using Specials and Prizes

Foursquare Specials are a built-in way to maximize the location-based service as a promotional tool for your library. Using Foursquare to offer deals for customers has been a major attraction of businesses to Foursquare since its inception. Libraries can also benefit from this added value. Coffee shops may offer discounts on lattes to customers who become mayor of their Foursquare venue, and restaurants can offer free appetizers as specials to attract and reward Foursquare-using customers. Libraries can similarly leverage this feature to reward and engage patrons who physically visit the library. In this

▶ Figure 5.3: Enter Your Verification Code

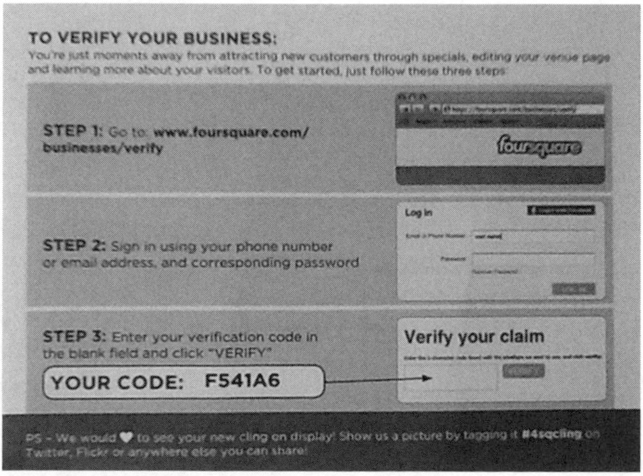

section we will talk about how to create specials and what types of specials are best for libraries to maximize this technology's benefits.

These are the major types of Foursquare specials you can use at your library:

- ▶ Specials for the library's mayor (the patron who checked in the most times in the past 60 days)
- ▶ Specials for patrons who check in at your library a determined number of times
- ▶ Specials for every time a patron gains a certain interval number of check-ins
- ▶ Open specials that you control with a free-text field and a process on your end

Foursquare specials can be created from the Add a Special tab on the venue page. Add a new special and designate if it's for the mayor or for any visitor who checks in a certain number of times, or input your own open reward. Once you submit your reward Foursquare will review it and, if it is approved, will send you details on how to make it active. You can manage established Foursquare specials from the "Campaign" page (see Figure 5.4).

Rewards for Mayorships

Mayorships form the backbone of Foursquare rewards. The now iconic Foursquare mayorship is a central motivator for many Foursquare users'

▶Figure 5.4: Add Specials to Your Venue

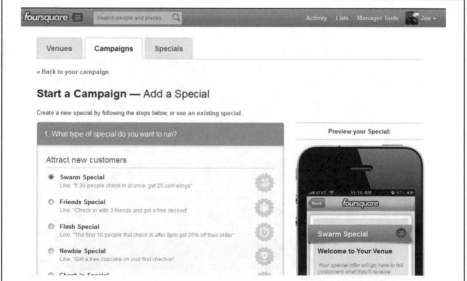

continued engagement. Any Foursquare user who checks into a Foursquare venue the most number of times wins the title "mayor" of that location. This brings with it several layers of rewards: the basic bragging rights of being crowned mayor, winning the in-game competition among Foursquare frequenters of that venue, winning competition against friends as a form of gaming, establishing a relationship with the real world and the digital representation of that location, and gaining possible physical rewards from the venue. Mayorship promotions offer a perfect way to reward frequent visitors to the library on a level that satisfies the patron in-game and in the real world.

Many places choose to do nothing to physically reward mayors, either consciously choosing to let the basic intangible benefits serve as sufficient or simply because of ignorance of this opportunity. There are many possible ways to reward the mayor of your library. Rewards can be tangible giveaways, gift certificates, or discounts or intangible rewards that offer benefits for the patron beyond Foursquare, such as offering a platform for their bragging rights by announcing the mayor across social media avenues to give them greater exposure and increase the audience of their bragging rights while serving to bolster a positive perception of the library as a social media PR strategy. Some examples of mayor rewards from the business world beyond libraries include Starbucks' offering a $1 discount off Frappuccino drinks and the Minneapolis–St. Paul Airport's program of rewarding mayors with a ball cap.

I suggest that libraries make sure to leverage the opportunity to reward patrons for engaging the library through mayor specials. Any way you do this is great. It needn't be grand or expensive. At the most basic level it can be a simple acknowledgment of the mayorship status. This can be in the form of reaching out in person and saying congratulations and thank you for visiting (identify them based on their profile picture or by contacting them), or it can be digital directly to their associated e-mail, their advertised phone number as a text message, their Twitter account as a Direct Message, or their Facebook page. Or your congratulations can be public, with the advantages of giving both them and your library wider acknowledgment and exposure, saying, in effect, "we love and reward our patrons, and we are hip because we use Foursquare!" Public acknowledgments can take the form of Twitter "@ replies," Facebook Wall posts on the library's Facebook Page or on the patrons' page, or comments in Foursquare on their winning check-in or as a comment in the activity thread announcing their mayorship. Any of these would be appreciated by the winners as long as it does not infringe on their privacy, is not done in an annoying manner, and does embrace the established social convention of the service. Some of these methods require additional steps: monitoring mayor turnovers, identifying Twitter feeds, friending patrons on Facebook and Twitter, and following patrons on Foursquare.

The options for libraries giving physical rewards include small tangible prizes such as coffee mugs or similar branded items or rewards with a monetary value like gift certificates or discounts to nearby or in-house businesses. The Darien (CT) public library rewards the mayor of its venue with a free tote bag.

Because libraries don't usually deal with physical objects the same way a business does, we have to consider what capital we do have to reward our social engagers. Libraries have the option of leveraging their operations as prizes by possibly waiving late fees as a reward for Foursquare mayors. Rewards may go well beyond physical prizes and enter more library-specific options, such as bumping a mayor up in the waiting line for a popular new release. Even dealing in knowledge as the prize is a viable option for libraries: reward mayors with inside tips to using the library.

Revoking Mayorships from Staff

Staff should not be allowed to compete with patrons for the Foursquare rewards offered by your library. Foursquare has a feature for venue managers to facilitate removing mayors if this should occur. You can remove the mayor of your library's Foursquare venue from the library's Foursquare page. On the right-hand side in the "Mayor" box select the reason for revoking, such as because they are an employee, or give another reason (if they won the mayorship unfairly or without actually visiting the library, for instance). Once you have selected to revoke the mayorship because they are an employee, they will no longer be able to compete to become the mayor. Alert your staff before doing this, explain to them why, and offer alternatives as discussed in the next project.

Other Rewards

Specials for patrons who check in at your library a preselected number of times is another great option. Rewarding anyone who checks in three times, for instance, is a positive way to keep library patrons who engage you on Foursquare interested and excited and is useful for expanding your library's rewards well beyond the singular mayor. These rewards can be smaller than those for mayors but should not be advertised less. It can be disheartening to users to not attain mayor status. So this method doubly serves to give users a sense of hope in their chances to get something more out of the game and to enhance your library's role in it.

Specials rewarded every time a patron gains a certain interval number of check-ins, every third check-in, for instance, is a great way to build customer loyalty. It is like getting a pat on the back for coming back repeatedly.

Open specials that you control with a free-text field and a process on your end as manager give libraries the maximum freedom for leveraging the

Foursquare rewards system creatively. Use this option to reward Foursquare users and build your social media presence. What you reward them for and with are entirely up to you. Think about some condition unique to your library or community that you can leverage as a reward or as a condition for earning it.

Create rewards with the rewards models on the venue page you manage. Select "Start a Campaign" and then "Add a Special," select which type of campaign, choose the variable if appropriate, and enter the conditions in the description field.

Group Rewards

Reward patrons for visiting in groups, such as classes, group project teams, reading clubs, or study groups, with the Friends special. Choose a number of friends, select a reward, and complete the reward form, for example, "Come to the library with four of your study group and enter a drawing to win a gift certificate." Patrons checking into your library with at least that many of their established Foursquare friends can claim the reward.

First Rewards

Reward patrons on a first-come, first-served basis with a Flash special to drive traffic at slower times: "The first five people to check in at the library after 2 p.m. this afternoon will win an iTunes gift card."

Swarm Rewards

Entice larger groups of not yet connected patrons to the library with the Swarm special. Select a number of patrons who visit in a specified three-hour time frame, and reward them all only if that many show up. For example, "If 15 people check in at the library before noon we will waive each of your overdue fines."

Newbie Rewards

Create a Newbie special to reward first-time visitors as a way of rewarding all patrons who come to the library, not just frequent visitors. Keep the reward small, but maximize prizes that give in-game rewards that make patrons feel welcomed.

Adding Tips

Once you have established a Foursquare venue, you can add Tips. Tips are like little recommendations or reviews added by anyone attached to Foursquare venues. They can serve as helpful information, such as, "free Wi-Fi on second level," for extended engagement with the venue; or marketing information, such as, "also check out our website at…" or "stop in out of the cold for a comfortable seat and warm coffee." Libraries can take advantage of this feature for three main purposes: marketing the library location to attract visitors, adding value to checked-in users' experience, and allowing for crowd input. Tips can pop up if users check in to nearby locations, so strategic and attractive tips can be great for getting local users' attention and bringing them in (see Figure 5.5). Adding tips about advanced features of the library is a great way to improve and deepen their experience with your library via Foursquare. Promoting tips contributed by patrons is a great way to have them expand the experience for themselves, and it's some free marketing for you.

Creating Badges

One of the most exciting rewards for Foursquare users is earning a badge. A Foursquare badge is a small but symbolic, much sought after in-game status reward given to users who check in at a designated spot or perform a designated action, usually repetitively. Badges usually consist of a branded icon and a small phrase (see Figure 5.6). Badges are either "core badges," created by Foursquare itself, or "partner badges" created in partnership

▶ **Figure 5.5: Foursquare Tips Screen**

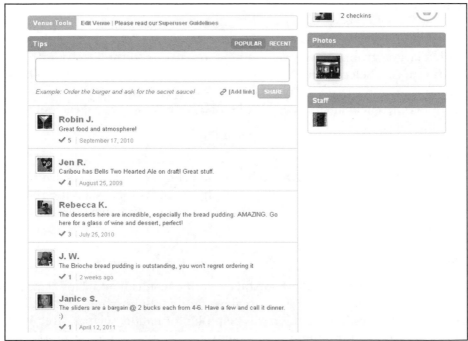

▶ Figure 5.6: Foursquare Page Request Form, One Step in Applying for a Badge

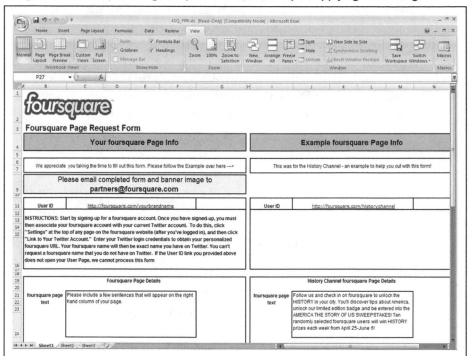

with outside brands. You can submit a proposal for a partner badge, but chances of getting it approved unless it meets Foursquare's own business needs are slim. Badges are earned by repeatedly visiting a designated venue or type of venue or by completing a series of tasks to drive users to engage those acts.

Libraries wishing to capitalize on this exciting part of the Foursquare experience may wish to create a badge that their users can win by engaging them through Foursquare. For instance, a badge could be earned by patrons if they visit each library in the system, or annotate and tweet a Foursquare check-in with a particular hashtag, or check in to designated locations. Unfortunately, Foursquare is not always open to working with smaller institutions for this type of branded reward. It is always worth periodically contacting Foursquare staff for an update, but, for the most part, it is not possible for small libraries to obtain custom Foursquare badges.

Another option is to have a branded presence in Foursquare. Harvard University, *Gossip Girl*, and *The New York Times* are each examples of corporate brands that have a presence on Foursquare as a formal way for them to share tips and favorite venues, and for libraries, a branded presence is the way to gather followers. This method allows for customer engagement and enhancing their Foursquare experience along the brand's terms. This also, however, is not available for libraries. This is too bad, because brands on Foursquare have the opportunity to create a custom page as a landing site on Foursquare, add tips, gain followers, and possibly create partner badges. There are ways to substitute these activities though. Your library venue has a page with some minimal options for customization. You can leverage websites on your own server for similar uses; adding a tip is something anyone can do, and followers are similar to fans.

Tracking Performance

Another fantastic benefit of claiming a venue as manager is that you have access to rich statistics about visitors' interactions with your library on Foursquare. Gathered statistics include total number of check-ins (see Figure 5.7), number of unique visitors, percentage of check-ins that are shared on Twitter and Facebook, and how many men versus women check in (see Figure 5.8). You can also view times of day of check-ins by percentage, most frequent users, and recent visitors. All of this data will come in handy when evaluating and assessing your library's Foursquare program.

► Figure 5.7: Basic Foursquare Venue Check-In Statistics

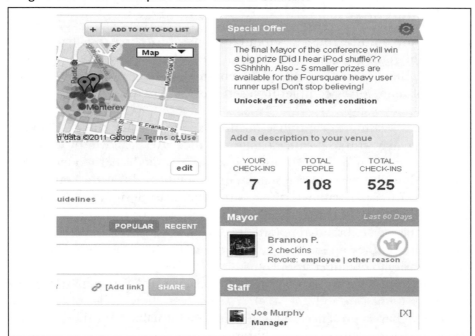

▶ Figure 5.8: Foursquare Statistics Page

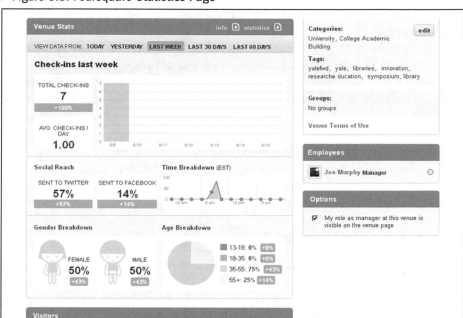

▶ USE FOURSQUARE TO SUPPORT STAFF WORK

There are several ways to use Foursquare for staff at your library. First, consider workplace policies for staff engaging Foursquare. Allow staff to check in on Foursquare at work, promote it as an acceptable behavior, allow the use of library equipment for Foursquare usage, and do not seek to block the use of personal technology by staff for these uses at the library.

Staff Venues for Rewards

Facilitate staff usage of Foursquare in ways that do not disrupt patron use and programs by creating staff venues on Foursquare for them to check in to. You can create special venues for each department's office or staff room and host a friendly competition among staff to be mayor, giving out prizes monthly to reward staff. You can create or encourage staff to create Foursquare venues for their own individual offices. This gives them a chance to be able to engage Foursquare at a workplace they frequent, earn points, and secure a mayorship. Other staff can even then check in to their coworkers' offices when visiting or during meetings. Individual library branches can have their own staff venue, such as "Staff of Downtown Free Library." This allows for staff check-ins and worker rewards programs and gives the opportunity for wider endeavors around which to build staff reward programs.

To implement venue check-ins, create the suggested venues for staff and encourage them to create their own that will best match their own experiences. Claim and manage the venues to manage rewards programs and control any staff versus patron check-ins. Clearly mark the venues as "for staff only" so that patrons do not attempt to check in to those venues. Beginning the venue title with "Staff" is the most effective method, because the full title often will not appear on mobile applications. If staff create the venues, ask that they maintain this or similar naming conventions.

Foursquare locations for staff should carry their own benefits. These staff venues can be great beyond the staff's own engagement. They can be used to create rewards programs.

Foursquare for Staff Learning Events

You can also use Foursquare locations for staff to access continuing education programs. Reward staff who attend and check in to professional development events on Foursquare by monitoring visitors to those locations or by having them post shout-outs about what they learned. Reward staff who engage the technology as early adopters and help their colleagues as well. Create multiple scavenger hunts to reward staff who attend multiple events or who make the effort to visit and network with relevant departments or branch locations. Library events are location specific; use that location as a leverage point.

Foursquare for Attendance Tracking

Foursquare provides an engaging way for staff to show that they attended an instruction class or continuing education event. Help staff set up a Foursquare account and have them check in at the proper venue to show their attendance. Make sure that the venue is clearly named and that its name is shared ahead of time. Foursquare is constantly updating and revising as a growing and dynamic company, so be sure to take a look at this book's companion website (http://www.alatechsource.org/techset/) for more details on Foursquare.

► USE FACEBOOK PLACES TO CONNECT WITH PATRONS

Facebook unveiled its addition to the location-based social phenomena, Facebook Places, in the summer of 2010. Facebook brought location-aware check-ins to a much higher level of visibility by opening Places up to its then 600 million users, cementing the role of location-based networking in our social lives. By putting the location check-in action within an established social network, Facebook Places also brings the location sharing activity directly into our social activity streams.

Facebook Places is streamlined within the mobile Facebook application. Users select "Places" in the application homepage or select "Check In" from the posting action bar at the top of the screen. They then scan a list or map of friends checking in nearby, click "Check In," and select their listed location (see Figure 5.9). While checking in, users can choose to add a comment about their check-in or tag friends who may also be there.

People use Facebook Places to share their location or activity with their Facebook social network just as they would share their status, photos, or links and reciprocally to see where their friends are. This integration into the established social graph, along with the social connections with people checking in and the Facebook pages they are checking into, make the location check-in process a primarily social activity.

Some people use Facebook Places for more than checking in. By browsing nearby locations, they use this location-based tool for local discovery, seeing what is nearby, and deciding where to go.

With Facebook Deals, a related promotion service, businesses can offer specials to users who check in. With Deals users can browse nearby locations to see which are offering promotional deals, check in, and show their phone to the cashier to claim and share with their friends. Facebook Deals claimed at your venue will be posted on the Facebook walls of the patrons who

▶ Figure 5.9: Check In to Facebook Places

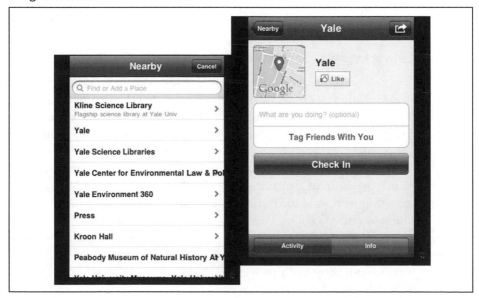

claimed them, advertising their engagement with the library to their social circles.

Claiming Your Library's Facebook Places Venue

Claim your library's Facebook Places venue to manage its representation, including address, contact information, image, open hours, and more.

Establish a Facebook account with which to set up Places for your library. You must have a Facebook account in order to utilize Places. Use a staff member's account or even a business Facebook account. Consider creating a joint staff account for this and related purposes that can be managed by various staff. If creating such an account, use a generic e-mail address that can be jointly managed. Consider who will have access to this e-mail account, and develop work flows for managing incoming Facebook content and notifications.

A Facebook Places page is created for venues when a person checks in or automatically from the Places directory. If no Places page exists for your library, create one through the mobile application, check in, search for your library by name, click "Add," and enter its name and description.

Claim your library's Facebook Places venue by clicking the "Is This Your Business" link on its Places page. Certify that you have the right to claim this location, and then claim through e-mail or with documentation. To claim by e-mail, make sure your library's e-mail address is added as a secondary e-mail account to your Facebook account. You will receive a notification from Facebook that the claim is being processed, and then you will be alerted by e-mail when the claim is approved. It may take several weeks. You can also claim the venue by providing proper documentation about ownership of the library.

Facebook Places versus Facebook Pages

When a Facebook Places page is created, it is not associated with an existing Facebook page. Rather, it creates a new one for the venue location. This can be a problem for libraries that have already created a Facebook page and invested energy into populating it and growing an interactive community on it. Many people may want to combine these in order to have one Facebook presence for their library, instead of two, to maintain. Unfortunately, it is not possible to merge them at this time. But there are benefits to having two. The most prominent reason for having a separate Places page is that it allows you to create and run Facebook Deals.

Libraries have a few choices about how to best address multiple pages. You can accept the duo Facebook Pages and maximize the strengths of each. This requires time invested on each page to populate the presence and create/ monitor patron interaction.

Another option is to focus purely on the new Places page and transfer your library's presence over to that portal. Brand this new page, and direct interaction toward it. Make the interactive experience as full as possible to tie in the location of the library to its virtual representation within Facebook.

Or, you may choose to focus your location-specific check-in strategies on other opportunities that may more closely align with your established Facebook endeavors. This may best include the newer feature of checking into Facebook events as well as checking into pages. This meets the patrons' expectation of being able to engage a location-related activity, and it meets your institutional need of providing a means to check in via Facebook with the physical library. The shortcoming of this approach is that, although it embraces the check-in driven activity within Facebook in a manner that addresses location and social engagement via a mobile phone, it does not directly engage Facebook Places itself, and thus it keeps the library's presence in that venue from reaching its potential. It also does not cash in on the benefits associated with Facebook Places, including Facebook Deals, or provide a presence in the hot commodity of a listing in the Facebook Places tab, and it requires extra work to associate Facebook Events with the library's physical presence, something that may not align perfectly with the reality of associated events.

If using both a traditional Facebook page and a Facebook Places page, make sure to maximize the unique strengths of the Places page to get the most out of your effort for your library. This includes adding all the information and interactive programs, links, services, and applications. Provide an image, full address, contact information, and both an official name and a more user-friendly name that the library may be known by. Add relevant details to your library's Facebook Places page. Don't let your Places page for your library lie empty.

Facebook Deals

Set up Facebook Deals at your library by first claiming your business's venue and then contacting Facebook Deals representatives at http://www.facebook .com/deals/business. You will be asked to fill out a form indicating your Facebook information, your business information, and information about your library's Facebook page. Facebook Places representatives will assist in setting up and promoting the deals.

An option to self-create Facebook Deals for your library is available in beta form to select locations. If this is available to you, the process for creating deals is quite easy from your library's Facebook Places page. First select which deal type you would like to create. Next, specify the description of the deal your library will be offering. Include a deal summary and instructions on how patrons can claim the deal in 50 and 100 characters each, respectively. Specify date ranges for the deal, the quantity of deal prizes you are offering, and whether each patron can claim just once or once every day if applicable. Your deal will be reviewed by Facebook staff, so allow two days before it goes live. Facebook offers four different types of deals.

Individual Deals

Individual Deals are basic rewards such as discounts when you check in. An example of this type of deal for your library is offering a free bookmark with any check-in. Set up an *Individual* Facebook Deal at your library to give out free bookmarks to patrons who show their mobile phone to staff at the circulation desk to prove that they have checked in to your library on Facebook Deals.

Friend Deals

With Friend Deals, you can tag your Facebook friends who are with you to claim a promotion meant for small groups. All of the tagged friends must be present to claim this type of deal. This type of deal is great for encouraging library usage by study or book groups. Set up a *Friend* Facebook Deal at your library to reward study groups who have claimed the Friend Deal you set up at your library who meet the number of friends you have specified to be the best group study area in your library.

Loyalty Deals

Loyalty Deals are meant to reward frequent visitors. Use Loyalty Deals at your library to reward patrons who have checked into your library multiple times on Facebook Places. This rewards them for being library users, as well as for engaging the technology at your library. Set up a *Loyalty* Facebook Deal at your library, and give patrons who have checked into the library four times a free pass on their next overdue book fine.

Charity Deals

Charity Deals are set up to offer a donation to a specified charity every time a visitor checks in. Use this type of deal at your library to drive donations for the local Friends of the Library group or local needs organization. Set up a *Charity* Facebook Deal at your library to donate two dollars to a disaster relief fund, local education improvement initiative, or library renovation fund every time a patron checks into your library on Facebook Places.

Deals That Target Library Patrons

Some suggested uses of Facebook Deals in your library include:

- ► rewarding frequent visitors,
- ► advertising events by offering rewards for attending, and
- ► giving out prizes to advertise the library.

Possible types of rewards to offer through Facebook Deals include:

▶ first choice of study rooms,
▶ discounts on late fees,
▶ a bump up in the waiting line for a popular item to check out, and
▶ a front row seat at an author's talk.

Make sure that all library staff, especially frontline service providers, are fully versed in the deals and the concept of Facebook Places. All circulation and reference staff should be fully aware and familiar with Facebook's mobile presence, trained on how Facebook Places is used, and instructed about what Facebook Deals are and how the library is using them. Make sure staff understand the criteria of the deals and know how to recognize and reward participating patrons.

Facebook offers best practices and suggestions for maximizing your deals:

▶ Discounts of 10 to 50 percent tend to work best. Translate this into 10 to 50 percent off of late fees.
▶ Keep deal titles and information brief to maximize the concise mobile space.
▶ Communicate all deals information with those who administer the program, including deal information, length of promotion, number of rewards being offered, and restrictions.
▶ Create a process for recording deals claimed.
▶ Keep the run time of deals short to maximize the interest.
▶ Run only a few deals at a time.
▶ Have a plan for scaling or expanding your deals.
▶ Populate the associated Facebook page and Places page.

Facebook has done a wonderful job adapting its products as the technology changes, making user interface changes to how locations are engaged. For more information from Facebook, see http://ads.ak.facebook.com/ads/FacebookAds/EMEA_partner_deals_businesses_EN.pdf; and visit the companion website (http://www.alatechsource.org/techset/) periodically to keep current on this topic.

▶ CREATE AN AUGMENTED REALITY PROGRAM IN YOUR LIBRARY

Imagine being able to peek at the extensive online information about real-world objects just by looking at them through your smartphone. View a shelf of books and immediately identify which items are out of order. Scan a house on the real estate market and see its selling price and complete history. Look at a piece of campus art and also view information about its creator. With augmented reality applications we can use our smartphones to access the vast world of digital information that is associated with the three-dimensional world in front of us. There is always more information than meets the eye.

"Augmented reality" refers to applications that put a layer of digital information on top of a view of a real-world object as seen through a mobile device or computer camera. Augmented reality programs commonly utilize the following three features of smartphones:

1. the location as determined by the gadget's internal GPS,
2. the direction the device is pointing toward usually ascertained by its accelerometer, and
3. the camera.

With these elements, the augmented reality program is able to identify where the viewer is, the direction where the viewer is looking, and what objects are in the view and then pull together and present relevant information associated with the place and the view. The digital information retrieved appears within the view of the object through the device's display screen and may seem to hover over the actual object.

One of the biggest barriers for adoption of augmented reality programs has been the technical requirements on the user's end. To use augmented reality programs, you need a mobile device equipped with an Internet connection, a camera, a GPS chip, and the ability to interact with the behind-the-scenes databases that feed information to augmented reality products. In short, an advanced smartphone or tablet computer is required to engage augmented reality. This has been a bit of a barrier to the technology's growth, as smartphone penetration has been too slow to drive high rates of adoption. However, there has been a remarkable shift in this trend recently. More and more consumers have smartphones, increasing the access to augmented reality products, and more people are becoming more familiar with such advanced uses of mobile devices.

ARSights (http://www.arsights.com/) uses premade augmented reality tags to display three-dimensional images of popular tourist sites. Toyota uses augmented reality tags to allow people to view and manipulate images of its new cars as well as take a look at its parts (http://vimeo.com/32071954). The 5gum augmented reality application for music allows for an interactive experience creating music (http://www.5gum.fr/?lang=en). The Virginia Museum of Fine Arts enhanced its Picasso exhibit with augmented reality by leveraging Layar to highlight select pieces in virtual space (http://mashable .com/2011/02/10/qr-codes-picasso/). Amsterdam's Allard Pierson Museum used augmented reality to reveal additional information about photographs of historical places (http://www.engadget.com/2009/04/13/augmented-reality-on-hand-at-museum-in-the-netherlands-threaten/).

Using Augmented Reality in Library Spaces

Engage the Virtual Graffiti augmented reality application in your library (http://itunes.apple.com/us/app/virtual-graffiti/id334564019?mt=8&ign-mpt =uo%3D6). Virtual Graffiti is an application that provides a way to add virtual graffiti art to your location. With this app you can add augmented reality signs in your library, enhance library signs, and encourage patrons to add their own signs or art. The strength of this application is that it allows for signs and art that don't exist in the real world to be visible via augmented reality (see Figure 5.10).

Create virtual signs within your library using the Virtual Graffiti app. Encourage staff to add simple "graffiti" art or signs around the library that they think may prove useful for patrons based on the common questions about highly used spaces they receive. Either supply a link to the application download for the staff to add on their own mobile devices or share a department- or staff-owned device for this purpose. Creating guerilla signs (nonofficial signage) in this manner can help streamline your library's ability

▶ Figure 5.10: Use Augmented Reality to Create Signs

to post up-to-date signage and not have to wait for signs to be created through the official channels. Also use Virtual Graffiti to add augmented reality versions and update existing library signs or flyers. Add humor, correct information, and keep signs up-to-date.

Encourage patrons to add virtual signs to your library. Patrons tend to know their needs and those of their peers well, so let them provide the signs they feel would be helpful for fellow library users. Ask them to use this application to add informational signs throughout the library. This gives patrons a sense of guerilla contributing and even adventure as a legal form of graffiti.

Create a virtual art exhibit within your library. Invite patrons and staff to use the library walls as the canvas for their artistic expression. Announce online and within the library that the library can be their venue for hosting artwork. Or encourage them to doodle on the walls while in the library. Also use this application to uncover patron feedback "written on the walls" and to generally provide an incentive to patrons who use augmented reality for engaging the library.

Promoting Augmented Reality Use for Learning

Engage the Pocket Universe augmented reality application in your library (http://itunes.apple.com/us/app/pocket-universe-virtual-sky/id306916838? mt=8). You can use this established augmented reality service within your library without having to create or modify tools. It displays astronomical information about the sky in your view and can enhance science education programs (see Figure 5.11).

Offer Pocket Universe as a reference resource to accompany other tools for stargazing and astronomical reference. Pocket Universe shows you the details behind your current view of the sky by using your location, direction, and your mobile device screen. Public libraries can use it to answer reference questions about the phases of the moon, constellations, spotting the International Space Station, and identifying current views of planets. School libraries can use it to teach about basic astronomy and stargazing and provide it to children as a hands-on learning tool. Academic libraries can provide it as a ready reference tool for answering questions about stellar objects' cataloged names or their brightness.

Creating Custom Augmented Reality Library Content

One prevalent augmented reality product, Layar, is already demonstrating the value and applications of the technology on a wide public scale. Layar describes itself on its Facebook page this way: "Layar is a mobile platform for discovering information about the world around you" (http://www.facebook

▶Figure 5.11: Image Created with the Pocket Universe Augmented Reality Application

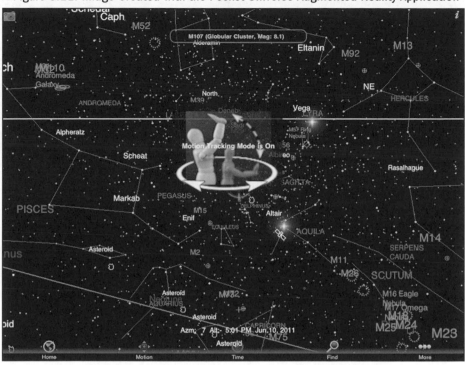

.com/augmented.reality.layar). Layar is a mobile application for iOS, Android devices, and Symbian mobile devices that allows you to use your mobile phone to display layers of digital information about objects in view.

To use Layar, download it, create an account, select layers, and point your device's camera at something to view information about the scene revealed by the selected layer. These are some popular layers:

> **Instagram:** Shows photos posted in Instagram that were taken around you
> **Tweeps:** Shows nearby Twitter posts that were associated with that location
> **WikipediaWorld:** Shows *Wikipedia* entries around you
> **Yelp:** Shows restaurant reviews and more
> **Weather AR:** Reveals the weather forecast for your location
> **Architecture 3D:** Pulls information from an international architecture database to show views of building projects

The major options for leveraging Layar at your library include encouraging use of existing layers and engaging Layar users and creating custom layers that make use of existing layers to contribute library-specific resources to the augmented reality program.

Encourage Use

Encourage the use of Layar in your library. The simplest way to use Layar in your library is to facilitate your patrons' own organic uses of the augmented reality app. Encourage patrons to use the app within the library just as they may outside of it. The goal of this is to bring the technology into the library, demonstrating that the library is a useful place to explore with the technology and that the library's policies are modern and welcoming to this new tool. Suggest that patrons use Layar to see Yelp reviews, Google Places information, and Foursquare check-ins at the library with those respective layers. Ask them to share with library staff and their social networks what they may learn about things in the library or the library building itself using Layar.

Engage existing Layar users. Bring Layar users into the library community and have the library enter theirs by asking patrons what their favorite layers are. Make this social by creating a Twitter meme with this question as a hashtag. Ask patrons to share their favorite layers with a Facebook question. Poll patrons about how they would like to be able to use Layar in the library by asking for suggestions for how they would like to use Layar with collections or services.

Create Custom Layers

Examples of more active approaches to leveraging Layar in your library include creating programs that use Layar within the library and creating custom layers to be added to Layar.

Create layers to be added to Layar. The ultimate application of Layar for your library would be to submit content in the form of custom layers that are of direct use to your library users. Types of layers to create include:

- ▶ historical data sets associated with geotagged locations;
- ▶ relevant image sets with location coordinates that have local historical value;
- ▶ history data and links for library, campus, and town buildings; and
- ▶ service, hours, and events information associated with library locations.

Developing custom information layers with Layar is an advanced project. It can be a simpler project, though, if you make use of the vetted list of developers that it offers. You may hire one of these expert developers, use one of the third-party tools they provide to directly create layers in, or use the detailed instructions that Layar provides for establishing yourself as an independent developer. If you choose to independently create a Layar developer account, there is plenty of help documentation provided for you at http://www.layar.com/development/make-layers/. The third-party tools provide their own instructions, and most require a fee (http://www.layar .com/development/tools/third-party-tools/).

Using Augmented Reality for Shelf Reading

You can use existing augmented reality services created specifically for library work, such as Shelvar (http://www.users.muohio.edu/brinkmwi/ar/). This is a shelf-reading augmented reality application produced by Miami University professor Bo Brinkman of the Miami University Augmented Reality Research Group. This application provides a unique staff work function by scanning a shelf of books and quickly alerting the user to which books may be out of order. It even goes one step further and recommends how to quickly reorder the books.

Shelvar works on Android devices and uses augmented reality tags that are encoded with the books' call numbers. It reads the tags on the binding of each book and projects a visible red X on those not in the correct order and a green check mark on those correctly shelved (see Figure 5.12). The service also helps reshelf misplaced books; tapping the screen over the view of an item marked as out of place will produce an arrow showing where the misplaced item should be moved to. As a side benefit, Shelvar can also generate

▶ Figure 5.12: Use Shelvar to Identify Incorrectly Shelved Books

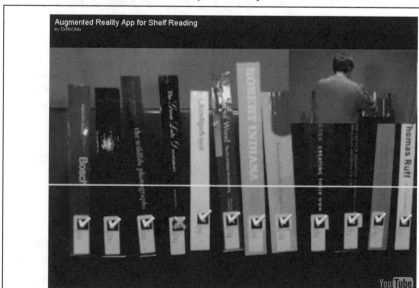

a list of the books scanned. This time- and money-saving service makes shelf reading more efficient, lessens the reliance on human eyes for error detection, and decreases the call number literacy training for shelf readers.

Shelvar is an example of how augmented reality can be a behind-the-scenes staff work technology, not only a frontline service tool. The application's creator plans to make it available for free for librarians in the future.

Other Uses of Augmented Reality in Libraries

Augmented reality is one facet of the larger trend impacting how, when, and where information is experienced. Just as with QR codes and Foursquare, augmented reality reflects the increasing importance of location as an element of information discovery. Libraries trying to stay relevant as a partner in the world of information access must move their resources and services into a mobile world beyond libraries, computers, and books and focus on the point of need being the point of engagement. Here are some further suggestions for libraries:

- ► Bring rare books to life without exposing the items to dangerous handling.
- ► Engage special collections with supplemental material and multimedia.
- ► Attach reviews to new or prominent books.
- ► Provide patrons access to the library's electronic resources for use beyond the library by adding links in augmented views of buildings, journals, books, posters, study guides, classroom whiteboards, and more.
- ► Augment reference services by bringing high-demand reference material into the view of a reference area.
- ► Augment instruction by associating teaching materials to areas or learning objects and providing access via augmented reality programs.
- ► Connect spaces or items with layers of digital information that expand the learning environment and provide more online information than would otherwise be available with that item.
- ► Expand orientation opportunities with augmented reality by adding digital layers to the library building or interior views with established or organic augmented reality programs. These can include orientation videos and visual tours.
- ► Place augmented reality tags on call number ranges that reveal an image associated with that topic.
- ► Leverage augmented reality to provide access to a building's history by ensuring that related online information about your library or other buildings can be attached to those objects via popular augmented reality programs.

▶ Enhance campus maps and tours with augmented reality services to bring the hidden but sought-after information into view for strolling students, parents, or visitors.

▶CREATE A LIBRARY QR CODE CAMPAIGN

QR codes are bar codes that hold more information than traditional bar codes and can be scanned with smartphone applications. They can contain customizable information, including links, text, and contact information.

QR codes are a location-based technology because they use a physical object or surface at a location as a point of access to link to digital information. I often refer to QR codes as a "mobile bridge" because of their ability to leverage mobile devices to connect real-world objects with the rich world of digital information. They are a form of hyperlinks for reality.

The major considerations for using QR codes in your library are:

▶ obtaining the technologies to create and scan them,
▶ determining the library services and programs that they can enhance,
▶ deciding the data they will link to or add, and
▶ assigning the staff to create and maintain them.

QR codes are useful because they allow you to access limitless digital information from a limited physical space, to link from a simple image to vast online information not available on site, and to store, access, and engage information directly through your smartphone without having to exit your mobile life flow. QR codes are included on advertisements to link beyond the print page to richer data and experiences. QR codes can be added to museum or library displays to link to more information about an author or artist.

I suggest adding QR codes to online subject guides, library information pages, librarian contact pages, database instructions and search tips, tutorials, and any other point where you want to enhance a digital presence with a mobile component. QR codes can be added to webpages, wikis, and blogs as image files or as embedded code.

Embed Contact Information in QR Codes

Create a QR code containing your library's contact information to add to library business cards, flyers, signs, and even webpages and social networking profiles. Create a QR code for your library's phone number, and patrons can scan the code and with one tap call the library or save the number to their contacts list. The benefit of this is that the patrons have access to your library through their smartphone without having to take any additional manual steps. With their phone they can scan your QR code, save your number, and reach out to you all from within a preferred mobile environment that you have made accessible from your physical library. Create signs with links to hours of operation and open/closed information to post on your library door or front window.

You can create a QR code at any one of several free QR code generator websites. QR Stuff (http://www.qrstuff.com/), Mobile Barcodes (http://www.mobile-barcodes.com/qr-code-generator/), and ZXing (http://zxing.appspot.com/generator/) are capable of producing codes in contact information format. For this purpose, we'll use the QR Code Generator from the ZXing Project at http://zxing.appspot.com/generator/. Go to this URL, and select "Contact information" in the Content dropdown menu to output your information in the proper format for displaying and storing contact information (Figure 5.13).

Use all of the available fields within the ZXing generator, including name, company, phone number, e-mail, address, and website. The Memo field can be used for including information that doesn't fit into the other fields, such as Twitter username or a subtitle or a note about the library.

Once created, choose the size of the code to export that best fits your planned usage. Remember that size of the code can affect the quality of the scan. For signs and posters, select "Large"; for business cards, e-mail

▶ Figure 5.13: QR Code Generator from the ZXing Project

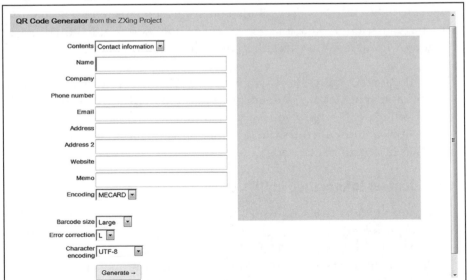

signatures, and other smaller display surfaces, select "Small." "Medium" will work well for most web displays.

Save the generated QR code as an image file. Right click the code image to Save As, or copy the provided HTML code for future use and for quick embedding into a webpage or blog.

Tip

Plan ahead of time for where you will save the files, and consider who should have access to the folder and if it needs to be shared via Dropbox or another cloud storage site. Work together with colleagues to develop naming conventions for the saved QR code files to maximize efficiencies in finding and identifying saved images.

Test Your QR Code

To scan QR codes you need a QR code scanner application for your smartphone just as users would in order to read or scan your bar code. You can purchase QR code scanning applications within your mobile carrier's application store. For QR code scanners, search the Apple App Store for "QR code" to download a good scanner application for the iPhone. I recommend QuickMark (http://www.quickmark.com.tw/En/basic/index.asp) and BeeTagg (http://www.beetagg.com/en/). For Android devices, QuickMark and Barcode Scanner (https://market.android.com/details?id=com.google.zxing.client .android&hl=en) come highly recommended. You can use your newly downloaded QR code scanner application to test the QR code you have produced for your library's contact information.

To scan your code, open the application and point your phone's camera at the code. Make sure the code is in focus and within the view limits. If using QuickMark, the code will scan automatically and its information will be displayed or opened. If using BeeTagg, select "Camera" within the application to begin scanning, and touch the camera icon to initiate the scan. The information you programmed into the code will appear displayed in its proper fields. If anything looks off, take this opportunity to regenerate the code to correct the error.

Post Your QR Code

You can post the QR code that you have created on visible flat surfaces around your library: as signs on the reference desk; within already posted hours signs; or taped to windows, doors, and index cards on shelving (see Figure 5.14).

QR codes are not limited to physical surfaces. You can also post them online as part of digital signage or on your library's website. The strength of

► Figure 5.14: Post QR Codes in the Book Stacks

posting QR codes online as images, even though the patrons are already in a linked environment when encountering the code, is primarily that the code then serves the purpose of bringing that linked data to their smartphone, freeing them and the information from the computer screen that displayed it. This is especially helpful with types of data useful for mobile patrons: links to Google maps, codes with SMS content, and any contact information. Links (especially to mobile webpages) are accessible to most patrons with smartphones. Also consider that the smartphone may be a popular access method to your library's website.

Create QR Codes Linking to Social Networks

Twitter

You can create a QR code to connect patrons with your library's Twitter account. Use the generator at http://zeek.com/create-a-status-update-url-for-twitter/ to create a link that leads patrons to their Twitter account via a mobile webpage and populates a Tweet with preselected text that can have them contact your library via a Twitter @ reply. The only step required of the patron is to push the "Tweet" button. Enter this link into a QR code, and you can have patrons contact you with a quick scan of the code.

Facebook

Facebook links to your library's Facebook page, Facebook profile, or Facebook Group can also be easily included in QR codes to facilitate easy mobile linking to your library's social presence. You can do this by using the open free-text fields in QR code generators with the contact information format or by just popping your Facebook's URL into one of these free-text format fields and as link codes. QR codes can also connect to the Like feature of Facebook to integrate the power of the Facebook Like button with physical media and surfaces. Facebook has sent out special custom window decals to some businesses that say "Like us on Facebook" and include the page's custom URL and instructions for how to Like a page by SMS (send the word "Like" followed by the Page name/URL as a text message to Facebook at 32665 if you have activated mobile Facebook on your account and device). This model can be expanded upon for your library by reproducing a similar flyer or sticker and adding a QR code with the same information or with a preprogrammed text message.

You can create QR codes to facilitate patrons Liking your library's Facebook page in several ways. You can simply enter your library's custom Facebook page URL into a QR code generator, print the generated code, and post it around your library, assuming patrons will take the action of Liking the page themselves. Or you can go a step beyond by creating a code with which your patrons can directly Like your page just by scanning it. One simple method for this is to use the generator at http://www.qrstuff.com/ to create a Like link code.

Create QR Codes for Library Instruction

If you provide instructional classes, you can distribute QR codes in the classes that have links to online handouts, instructional videos, and any other additional resources you taught about.

Posting QR codes that include instructions can be a great way of addressing problems that patrons frequently encounter. QR codes with a few sentences explaining how to print or use the copier can save a lot of headaches. Include links to instructional videos to provide even more help. This method can also apply to any operation for patrons at your library that can generate confusion: signing up for computer usage, getting a library card, paying library fines, placing items on reserve, accessing items on reserve, requesting books through interlibrary loan, and so forth. QR codes can provide help at points of need, especially where problems can be anticipated and staff are not available.

Create QR Codes That Link to the Library's Website and Catalog

To create a QR code that contains a link to your webpage or library catalog, just grab the desired URL and insert the URL into the proper field of any of the QR code generators mentioned in this chapter, generate the code, export it as an image, and post it as a flyer or a digital sign or on a webpage. When scanned, a QR code with a link will display the webpage.

Post signs in special sections of your library with QR codes that link to websites highlighting particular resources or topics. Enhance call number ranges in your library with QR codes on flyers that link to e-book collections on that topic. Add QR codes to print volumes or monographs that link to digital editions of that title. Create posters with QR codes that link to useful or fun resources for Young Adult areas. Post a QR code next to a library book that leads to a review of that book (see Figures 5.15 and 5.16).

Create QR Codes for Events

Create QR codes for events your library is hosting that contain date/time information by inputting the name of the event, its date and time information, the time zone, and the location using longitude and latitude. This can be done in vCalendar format at http://www.qrstuff.com/. Another generator, ZXing (http://zxing.appspot.com/generator/), also offers a calendar format as well as an additional description field and an open location field instead of coordinates. These options are great when the code is posted alongside

► **Figure 5.15: QR Code That Provides a Book Review**

▶Figure 5.16: Book Review Accessed by a QR Code

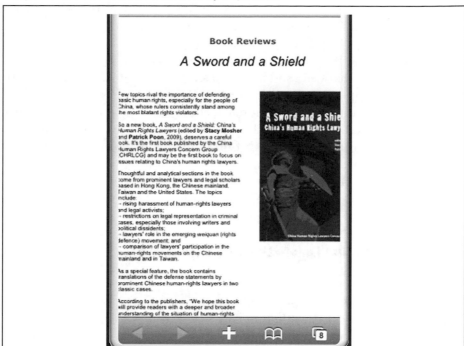

flyers advertising classes, on posters and online calendars, on brochures and handouts, and in newsletters or e-mails that advertise events.

Create QR Codes for Reference Services

QR codes can also be used to expand live reference services. Reference phone numbers and e-mail addresses are easily input into QR codes to enhance the service by literally putting the point of contact at patrons' fingertips. Include IM reference screen names in QR codes with the text format (such as with the Kaywa generator at http://qrcode.kaywa.com/). Use the SMS as a content option (provided by several QR code generators).

Create QR codes that pre-fill text messages that can be sent from patrons to the library's designated cell phone number; having the wording in the message field already entered will get the patron started. This option is great for libraries offering text messaging reference. Use this to enhance your SMS reference program by creating codes at http://qrcode.kaywa.com/ or http://delivr.com/qr-code-generator that include your SMS reference phone number and a bit of information that will help with the reference transaction. Be conscious of the character count limit, and keep the message simple. You may, for instance, include some text to prod the user toward including helpful information, such as, "my university ID is ___," or "my e-mail for follow-up is ___," or "I am texting from ___."

You can also use the website at http://delivr.com/qr-code-generator to create a QR code that will send a text message to a mobile phone–friendly short code as opposed to a full phone number. This is very useful for libraries that avoid staff usage of mobile technology but offers SMS reference through an Instant Message mashup or an SMS service that requires the inclusion of a username in the body of the text message on top of the short code address in order to be contacted. Include the IM service's universal short code for the desired service in the appropriate field, identify whether it is an IM client or another service, and enter your library's unique username into the Keyword field.

Create QR Codes That Link to Location-Based Services

Foursquare

QR codes can be used in conjunction with location-based services. Use the website at http://phi2.mobilelifecentre.org/ to create a QR code that patrons can scan to check directly into your library's Foursquare venue. The code you generate at this website can be used by patrons with an Android device and the φ^2 Scanner app to directly check in. This allows users to skip the step of searching or browsing for your venue in Foursquare and ensures that they check in to the proper venue, helping funnel check-in statistics, control duplication of venues, and focus Foursquare activity to best enable social connections. This product's method is unique for how it physically connects the real-life venue with the Foursquare location in the check-in process, putting the patron and the mobile phone as the only intermediaries.

Another method of connecting QR codes and location-based check-ins is to create QR codes that include links to or names of the library's Foursquare venue. It is likely that Foursquare users at your library will be checking in with a mobile application, so the link would be less helpful than a code with text that includes the name of the venue as it appears in Foursquare so they will recognize it or accurately search for it quickly. Input text similar to this example into a QR code generator: "Foursquare user? Check in to _____ Public Library and see if you can claim the Mayorship!"

Facebook Places

You can also leverage QR codes for facilitating patrons' checking into your library on Facebook Places with a mobile-friendly URL for your library's

Facebook Places location (at http://goo.gl/3rBPH, for instance). The URL should be in the mobile format, such as in this example: http://touch.face book.com/?w2m#/profile.php?id=XXXXXX&t&latitude=XX.XXXXXX& longitude=-XX.XXXXXXXXX. Replace the Xs with your library's unique ID, latitude, and longitude. You can find your library's latitude and longitude coordinates on its Facebook Places page.

Customize a shortened URL for your library's Facebook Places with Bitly or a similar service to brand the link. Patrons scanning this code will be taken to your library's mobile-friendly Facebook Places webpage from which they can easily Like or check in to your library. Post this code throughout the library and by the circulation desk so that patrons can check in while checking out.

Other Cool Library QR Code Project Ideas

The QR code's ability to link print items or other objects in the real three-dimensional world to online information is its central strength. A QR code can include a URL that links directly to any web address that contains, for example, an online video, a subject guide, a library homepage, a Twitter account, a Facebook page, a Google search page, an e-book, an OPAC record, a mobile application to download, a *Wikipedia* article, or a webpage with instructions for a research resource. Here are a few more project ideas:

- ▶ Post QR codes in digital signage or print posters with:
  - ➤ instructions for in-library operations and tools,
  - ➤ links to instructional videos,
  - ➤ links to electronic collections that accompany a collection in your library, and
  - ➤ links to author websites and additional item-related resources.
- ▶ Add QR codes to business cards for librarians.
- ▶ Embed QR codes in your website with links to subject guides links or to map directions.

▶ CREATE A GOWALLA MARKETING INITIATIVE FOR YOUR LIBRARY

Gowalla has long been a favorite location-based service with a loyal following and a strong user interface. Gowalla was one of the first major popular location-based social networks created for checking in and sharing your location. In essence, it is similar to Foursquare: you check in to your location, share that activity with friends, and add optional comments and pictures. With Gowalla, however, you can also create Trips, which are a series of locations tied together for a larger purpose. For example, you can create a Trip that includes all the branches of your library. Businesses market their brands using custom icons and rewards in Gowalla to increase purchases. Gowalla has a lot of potential for deeper patron interaction and offers more flexibility in promotion campaigns than some of the other location-based services.

Some uses of Gowalla for your library include the following:

► Marketing events
► Promoting services
► Driving traffic to the library
► Enhancing patrons' virtual experience at your physical library
► Viewing and responding to patron feedback

Creating an effective Gowalla marketing initiative for your library will entail careful planning for creating or leveraging a Gowalla account; creating and maintaining Gowalla Spots; connecting with patrons through Gowalla; leveraging Gowalla Bookmarks, Trips, Notes, and Highlights; and making the most of rewards within Gowalla. Understanding and applying each of these elements will add up to the whole of an effective marketing initiative with Gowalla for your library that will advertise the library's relevancy and its valuable specific services and resources.

Create a Gowalla Account

Create a staff account to access the rich features of Gowalla. I believe that you should not create an organizational library account for Gowalla but rather create an individual account for staff because buildings and institutions cannot add value to the social Gowalla experience of our patrons. Create an account in the mobile application by downloading it and entering the required information or associating it with a Facebook account. Be very clear who or what the account represents in the fields for name, e-mail, brief profile biography, and links to your website and social media accounts. Select a profile picture that includes staff faces so that patrons know they are connecting with people.

Gowalla Spots

Create a Spot on Gowalla for your library if one does not already exist. A Gowalla Spot is a representation of your library, just as a Facebook Places page or a Foursquare venue is. Suggested best practices include choosing a clear title that is recognizable by patrons and consistent with online and offline usage. Include a short, clear, and explanatory description. Choose the correct category for your library's spot: for academic libraries choose the parent category "College & Education" and the subcategory "Library"; public libraries should choose "Art & Culture" and "Library." Make sure the location of the spot you are creating is accurate at the next step. Gowalla will let you view on a map where your phone's GPS says the spot is. Drag and drop the Pin to the correct location if needed.

Connect with Patrons

Find and friend identified and potential patrons by synching your account with Facebook, Twitter, Gmail, Yahoo!, and Hotmail, and friend patrons you are already connected with in those networks. Friend patrons who check in to your library's spot, and market the account in e-mail signatures, on contact pages, and on social media accounts. Be prepared to respond to friend requests from patrons and accept all friend requests except from obvious spam accounts.

Promote Gowalla Bookmarks

Encourage patrons to bookmark your library's Gowalla spot to quickly find and check in to it as a way of making their experience most efficient and maximizing check-ins to your spot. Promote the Bookmark option through Tweets, flyers, and a check-in comment.

Market the Spot

Market your library's Gowalla Spot with the "Share This" button on the Spot page. Send it to your Twitter and Facebook accounts. Post a link to the spot in the address or direction sections on your website, Facebook page, and business cards.

Leverage Gowalla Trips

Gowalla Trips are a series of spots you group together to encourage or reward visits to multiple locations related to theme or task. Trips can include as many as 20 or as few as three spots. Library trips can include multiple campus or branch libraries or local/campus locations of use to patrons. Share the trip with your Gowalla friends, and publish it publicly on Twitter and the like or keep it private as an incentive for patrons to friend you. Trips can be created on a mobile application or easily online at http://gowalla.com/trips. Give it a clear name, assign a category, add a clear description, and include a link in the URL field to a corresponding blog post for more information.

To add spots to a trip, click the blue "Add a Spot" button or add it from any spot's venue page. Set the trip's "Check-In Requirements" to either all spots or a certain number of included spots visited. Choose a few, but not all, of the spots visited as the requirement to lessen barriers to patrons completing the exercise. Note that there is a limit of ten trips that you can create, so plan to maximize a small number of trips and delete trips when they become irrelevant. Reward patrons who complete the trip, and market trips online and in person in instruction and orientation sessions.

Add Highlights

Highlights are selected visual thematic tags for locations that "tell a story about a place that is special to you." Highlights are attached to Gowalla Spots by visitors who assign one of several premade highlight icons appropriate for the location that reflects the value they personally associate with that venue.

Add one or more appropriate highlights to your library's spot that will indicate a deeper, more personal or entertaining attractive value of your library. Ask patrons to add highlights to the spot, and monitor what they add for insight into how they view the values of your physical library space (see Figure 5.17).

Leave a Note at a Spot

Use Gowalla's Leave a Note feature at Spot pages for your library for specific friends that they will see when they check in to that spot. On a Gowalla Spot

▶ Figure 5.17: Encourage Patrons to Add Highlights to Your Gowalla Spot

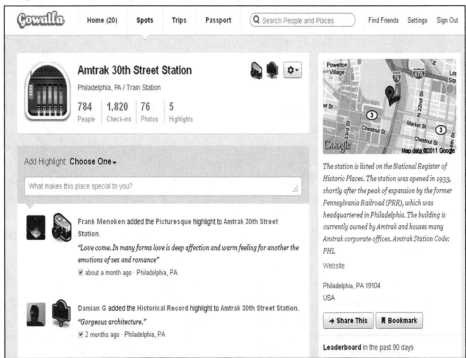

page, select the note option in the pulldown menu, choose which of your friends to leave it for, and enter the note in 300 or less characters. Leave notes for patrons who have specific research interests or for regular users you would like to reward with inside information. Use this feature's exclusivity as a draw to encourage patrons to friend you by leaving them advertising notes pointing out that patrons who friend the library on Gowalla will have access to elite tips.

Gowalla Rewards

The rewards system in Gowalla includes pins, items, points, and stamps. When patrons check in to your library they will win the generic library stamp that will be added to their passport.

You can purchase a custom stamp from Gowalla for your library to stand out and make this reward more relevant. Visit the stamps page (http://gowalla.com/stamps) to request one. The cost structure is affordable for libraries.

▶ CREATE A LOCATION-BASED PHOTO STREAM FOR YOUR LIBRARY

Mobile photo-sharing applications, including Instagram (a front runner with two million users), picplz, Hipstamatic, and Path, allow users to take, manipulate, and share pictures and associate them with location information through a mobile application. News publishers and other companies are leveraging Instagram to expand discovery of their stories and services and to add a social visual element. The power of Instagram for libraries lies in its ability to share and engage visual content in real time. Libraries can use Instagram to expand social media campaigns into a visually based mobile community to:

- ▶ enhance on-site events or displays,
- ▶ highlight collections or projects in the library with an image element,
- ▶ bring local user-generated content into the library's resources, and
- ▶ expand local discussions with related images.

In this project, we will leverage the Instagram mobile photo-sharing application to display patron-created photos of the library on the library's website through an RSS feed. We will use Instagram's application programming interface (API) to bring images together and to provide opportunities for patrons to contribute to the visual narrative of the library. In pursuit of leveraging Instagram's powerful suite of location-aware technologies for the library, we will create an account, apply and utilize hashtags, engage the Instagram API to highlight images, and promote the program through QR codes.

Create an Instagram Account

Instagram has no web presence and is currently limited to iPhones. Create an Instagram account for your library with the library's iPhone or with one belonging to a staff member. Choose an e-mail account to associate with your new Instagram account that will be findable by patrons who may already have the library in their contact lists. Create an easily identifiable username that clearly represents the library and reflects its established brand. Make it findable by patrons searching within the application and consistent with your library's other social media identities. Add a profile picture that uniquely identifies your library and is recognizable in small thumbnail format. Connect the new account to the library's Twitter, Facebook, Flickr, and Tumblr accounts.

Encourage Patrons to Take Photos

Instagram enables users to take photos with their iPhones and attach location information to the photos they've taken. Encourage patrons in your library to snap pictures of the library building, of their friends and themselves at the library, and so forth, with Instagram. Tell them that their pictures will be added to your website's wall of fame! Encourage them by posting flyers in the library with the message that it is okay to take pictures at the library and that users should tag the location with something like "this spot makes for a great pic" or "the lighting in this area is perfect for self-portraits." Also post pictures you take of these flyers to Instagram itself as a marketing technique that makes use of the activity you are encouraging. Post a note or status on your library's Facebook page that says "send your Instagram photos of the library to Facebook and tag the library in the caption."

Use QR Codes to Promote Your Instagram Program

Use QR codes to extend and market your Instagram program. Include a free-text QR code with photos or other image-based displays in your library that invites interaction about the display. It can say, for instance, "comment on this image in our Instagram stream, our username is ___." Or create QR codes that link to an RSS feed of your library's Instagram stream or to a feed that gathers pictures with a certain hashtag or from a location. Use Instagram to share image files of QR codes.

Use Hashtags to Bring Together Local or Related Images

A hashtag is a useful piece of metadata that users can add to their photos in Instagram in the photo title or caption. Hashtags can describe a subject, place, person, or thing just as an ordinary tag would. However, by prefacing the tag or descriptor with the pound sign, #, it makes it searchable and findable by that keyword within Instagram. It also enables the library, as well as users, to view streams of photos that have been similarly tagged. You can search and view all images with the same hashtag by clicking the tag in a caption or by searching for it with the "Search Instagram" feature in your Instagram profile page. Display collected images with the tag by saving the view of all related pictures with a screenshot and posting that image within Instagram and elsewhere, such as Facebook and Twitter, to advertise pictures at your library. Hang a poster of the images in your library to market the idea of patrons adding their own images about the library to the online community.

Hashtags that have already been added to Instagram pictures are searchable within the application, or you can tie together related images of your library or of a topic by adding hashtags to posts by you, by the library, or by library users simply by adding a comment to an Instagram post in hashtag format, with the pound sign # preceding an established or original tag. Types of pictures to add tags to include pictures with a relevant location element such as local history or a campus research topic or a homework or course work project, or simply tie together images to add pictorial value to a location-sensitive social media campaign. See Figure 5.18.

▶ **Figure 5.18: Use Hashtags to Find and Promote Images of Your Library**

Employ user-generated content to populate a display in the library or online. Seek submissions by asking patrons to post images in Instagram with a particular hashtag. Pull together pictures with that tag to create the display. The display can be hosted within Instagram itself, on a webpage or blog, or with pictures printed using Instaprint, the "location based photo booth for Instagram" (http://instaprint.me). The topic of the display can be "show us what the library means to you" or "post a picture of the cover from your favorite book." Searching for and adding hashtags within Instagram can also be activities your library can use to teach patrons how to use this tool.

Collect Your Photo Stream with RSS

Create RSS feeds from Instagram content. These RSS streams can be from a particular Instagram user or collected with a hashtag. Create RSS feeds from:

- library patrons,
- popular or local authors,
- local entities,
- the library and/or librarians, and
- the campus or town.

RSS feeds from Instagram users can be created with third-party services such as Heroku that use the Instagram API to provide access to posts. You just enter the username into the RSS feed URL—http://instagram.heroku.com/users/username—where it says "username." These RSS feeds can then be streamed onto webpages, hosted within subject guides, and used to feed blogs. You can also suggest that patrons add the feeds to their blog readers.

RSS feeds of Instagram hashtags can also be created to pull together related content beyond the application. These RSS feeds can be created by entering the hashtag into this URL: http://instagr.am/tags/hashtag/feed/recent.rss. Replace "hashtag" with the tag you would like to create a feed for. Tag RSS feeds can feature:

- current local news topics;
- current events of interest to subsets of patrons;
- posts related to popular books;
- posts from a timely event, conference, or awards show; and
- research topics.

An Instagram stream of images taken at your library can be created with one of several methods. You can pull together images tagged with the location as a hashtag (this method will cover images associated with the resources of your library and not just the building). Use the "More photos at this location" function at http://www.gramfeed.com or the map feature at http://extragr.am/ to display and gather images at your library as a location and then create an RSS feed of that page with a free RSS builder such as Feedity (http://feedity .com/) or Page2RSS (http://page2rss.com/). You can also bring together and create a feed of images taken at or near your library using the "Locations" and "Geographies" components of Instagram's API. This API method requires a more advanced project that can be started by registering your application with Instagram.

Manage Location Information Quality

Instagram allows you to share the pictures that you upload beyond its application to other services, including Foursquare, Flickr, Twitter, and Facebook. One way to leverage location with Instagram is to share posts to Foursquare. This checks you into the Foursquare location identified and adds the image to the Foursquare venue. You can monitor Instagram images posted by patrons to your library's Foursquare venue.

To post and share images to Foursquare you must associate your Instagram account with a Foursquare account. If using a staff member's Instagram account or an account for the library on a staff member's iPhone, connect it to the library's official Foursquare account as a parallel representative account. Your library can also create and log in to an Instagram account using a staff member's iPhone, but remember to log out first.

Manage the quality of the location information through Foursquare so that it is best represented within Instagram. Leverage the streams of other users or topics to enhance topic resources with visual location elements. Ensure that images of or associated with your library have accurate location data to maximize your library's presence by editing, if necessary, the metadata of your library's Foursquare venue.

▶ LEVERAGE SOCIAL RECOMMENDATION AND LOCAL DISCOVERY SERVICES

Personalized filters and social recommendations can complement hyper local discovery in very practical ways. When we want recommendations we want immediate information about what is nearby, we want the information filtered to suit our timely interests, we want it to reflect our preferences, and we want input from trusted peers. Local recommendation services such as Alfred and Bizzy make use of this confluence to provide personally relevant local recommendations based on user input from mobile interfaces. Your library can make use of these location-aware tools to maximize its visibility in this social discovery layer of mobile and web-based searching.

Create an Alfred Account

Alfred is an app that recommends nearby venues based on category and curated recommendations (see Figure 5.19). Alfred, developed by Clever Sense, Inc., is advertised as "your personal robot who recommends places based on your favorites" (at http://www.alfredmobile.com/) and is called the "Pandora for the real world" (at http://www.thecleversense.com/).

You get relevant recommendations by "Teaching" Alfred about your favorites; this involves answering questions about your preferences. Depending on your answers to such questions as "What is one of your favorite breakfast places on the weekend?" Alfred returns with suggested venues in other categories that you can give your approval to. This feedback helps populate the recommendations Alfred gives you when browsing for nearby venues. Alfred tells us, "The more you teach me, the smarter my recommendations will get." You can return to teach Alfred more at anytime or browse without signing in and teaching to immediately use. Returned results based on chosen category and your feedback are useful and accurate and provide detailed venue information, including contact information, location, reviews, photos, and

▶ Figure 5.19: The Alfred App

menus when available. You also have an option for further refining feedback by giving a thumbs-up or thumbs-down for each returned result.

Create a Bizzy Account and Connect

Bizzy, a prominent social recommendation engine, provides nearby suggested venues based on input from you and your social connections. Bizzy says, "Tell us your favorite places and we'll help you find new ones," and returns recommendations specifically filtered for you based on the venues you have added as favorites and those you've selected from their questionnaires.

Create a Bizzy account for your library or for a representative staff member with your library's location as determined by postal code and a library e-mail address. A staff account can be created by logging in with Facebook. Associate the account with Facebook and Twitter to maximize its full reach and social impact. Use your Bizzy account to ensure that your library is socially discoverable and recommendable. Make sure the account you use to do this is clearly marked as library staff to be transparent. Connect with patrons in Bizzy, and use it to make sure your library is included in the recommendations provided by the tool.

Use Quick Add and Favorite

Engage Bizzy as a staff member from the user's perspective. "Quick Add" your library's venue in Bizzy to increase its presence in the social graph and to bolster your account's ability to recommend the library within its social circles. On Bizzy, the number of "Favorites" a venue receives is displayed and can factor into a personal ranking of that place.

Answer Bizzy's Questions

Answer Bizzy's questionnaire about local venue references to build a list of associated venues. Insert your library as an answer to Bizzy's questions about places you like for specific uses wherever appropriate to populate your recommendation engine and thus extend the reach of your library as a potentially recommended venue (see Figure 5.20). Be creative in what arenas your library can qualify as an answer—it might be a good place to get a coffee as well as a spot for quiet study or Wi-Fi use.

Encourage User Reviews

Patrons can add tips and reviews to the Bizzy venue, monitor posts on your library's venue, and respond to complaints or questions. Add information in the "Posts" field, and send these tips to Twitter and Facebook as marketing for the library and for its usage of Bizzy. Posts can help browsers decide to visit your venue.

▶ Figure 5.20: Recommend Your Library on Bizzy

Advertise

Advertise your Bizzy venue within and beyond your library, and encourage patrons to Favorite it with Twitter, Facebook, blog posts, signs at building exits and throughout the library, and flyers outside of the library at community spots where people are already likely to use Bizzy. Use Bizzy itself by sending your venue to Facebook or Twitter. This will appear as the tweet "Get @Bizzy with (name of the library) Link #getbizzy." On Facebook it will post to your Wall as "I love (Library Name) http://www.bizzy.com/pub/business/_____. (Library Name) is blowing up on Bizzy. Come see what the hype is about!" Advertisements can include the Bizzy emblem, the library's name as it is spelled on its Bizzy venue, and a note to Favorite the library.

Reward Patrons

Reward patrons for engaging your library on Bizzy as a way of encouraging your users to market the library. Provide tangential or feedback rewards for favoriting and checking out at the library venue. Especially provide encouragement on Facebook and Twitter for those who send their interaction with your library to Bizzy.

Use Bizzy as a Checkout Service

Bizzy introduced a "Checkouts" feature in March 2011 to occupy a new space in location engagement beyond the discovery stage and the check-in. Bizzy

Checkouts allow users to engage a venue while at the location after checking in by saying they are at the location and giving feedback on their experience with a simple rating system of smiley, basic, and unhappy emoticons. Bizzy Checkouts give patrons an opportunity to engage your library's location after the Foursquare check-in in a way that can serve as positive marketing for the library. Your library can leverage Bizzy Checkouts to increase the social reach of your library's discoverability, to give patrons an opportunity to engage the place and add their input, and to collect usage data and feedback.

Users can browse how many positive or negative Checkouts a venue has received, so increase your library's discoverability in Bizzy and the value of the social recommendations it receives by adding positive Checkouts to your library so it rises in your social graph. Add Checkouts from staff and library accounts with helpful comments.

Encourage patrons to market your library by helping them use Bizzy Checkouts while at your library. Market the feature and the library's venue name and encourage them to Checkout "with a Smile," or to "Checkout on Bizzy while checking out books."

Collect feedback from patrons visiting your library by monitoring the values they attach to their Bizzy Checkouts and the Tips they add. You can respond to comments if they include questions or suggestions for improvement but also just to say thank you for engaging.

Leverage Bizzy's Follow Feature

Maximize Bizzy's option of following fellow users to see and interact with their check-in stream. Get patrons to Follow your library back so you share in the location engagement community. If your patrons Follow your library's account they will receive a push notification when you comment on their Checkouts at your libraries, putting your library on their mobile screen.

▶ IMPLEMENT A MOBILE PAYMENT SERVICE WITH GOOGLE WALLET AND NEAR FIELD COMMUNICATION AT YOUR LIBRARY

Accept library fine payments with the quick wave of a cell phone. With near field communication and Google Wallet, your library can easily easy accept mobile payments and offer rewards through Google's Offers program and mobile loyalty cards.

Near field communication is the next major wave in mobile activity for sharing content, making payments, and interacting with real-world networked objects. Google makes use of this burgeoning field by combining it with popular methods for interacting with a location.

Near Field Communication

With near field communication, also known as NFC, you can make quick and secure transactions by touching or bringing your smartphone close to an NFC reader or another NFC-enabled smartphone. NFC is a contactless technology that allows for simple wireless transfers of information or data collection across very short distances.

NFC is similar to QR codes in that both technologies involve transferring data into a smartphone, are ways of interacting with the physical world around us through our mobile phones, and necessitate close proximity. A major difference between NFC and QR codes, however, is that the latter require a visual element in the form of the QR code image as well as the phone's camera and a QR code scanner app. NFC requires smartphones that are built to include an NFC chip (stickers containing add-on NFC chips may soon be possible) and an NFC reader.

Another similar contactless technology is Radio Frequency Identification (RFID). The major difference between NFC and RFID is distance. NFC generally has a range of only four inches and has a bit more security.

With NFC, smartphones can be used in mobile payment transactions by touching them together or by tapping one against an NFC reader. NFC-enabled smartphones can also be used for sharing contact information, file swapping, or exchanging data with real-world objects.

There are other uses of NFC as well. Nokia released a speaker system, the Nokia Play 360°, that connects to a phone via NFC to play music on that phone. A few uses of NFC for your library include:

- ► accepting mobile payments with Google Wallet,
- ► accepting mobile payments with PayPal,
- ► facilitating e-book downloading,
- ► sharing contact info,
- ► providing instruction, and even
- ► offering scavenger hunts.

Google Wallet

Google recently unveiled a new product, Google Wallet, that uses NFC technology to make payments by tapping a smartphone on an NFC reader. Google Wallet can store your Citi MasterCard credit card information in your phone and allows you to use it to make payments at participating businesses. With the Google Prepaid Card you can add value to any credit card, making this service available to every type of credit card. Google Wallet also works with coupons and will soon offer loyalty cards. Google Wallet is available only on Nexus S 4G phones and is expected to expand to other Android devices soon.

You make payments with Google Wallet by tapping your smartphone on the PayPass terminal after the transaction is rung up by the cashier (see Figure 5.21). You can also redeem some Google Offers through Google Wallet at businesses that participate in Google SingleTap. As a merchant, Google Wallet does not require additional costs above that of normal credit transfer machines except for securing contactless terminals.

Use Google Wallet at your library to:

▶ collect fines and fees,
▶ accept payments for book sales,
▶ facilitate mobile donations, and
▶ facilitate Google Offers programs and mobile library loyalty cards.

Set Up Google Wallet at Your Library

To become a Google Wallet–accepting institution, contact Google at https://services.google.com/fb/forms/walletpartnerinquiry/. On the webform you will get, provide your name and contact info, choose "other" as Company Type, and include a note about your library.

For more information on business use of Google Wallet, go to http://www.google.com/wallet/merchants.html (see Figure 5.22). You will also need an NFC contactless pay terminal. You can get one from First Data by calling 888-265-8147 or by visiting their website at https://www.empsebiz.com/googlewallet/contact.php?cmpid=GWALLET.

All library staff should be trained on how to use the system, and they should understand its value and its role in the larger technology and consumer

▶ Figure: 5.21: Google Wallet Payments

www.google.com/wallet/#payments

► Figure 5.22: Google Wallet Merchants

landscape. Staff who will be performing point-of-sale operations should be trained in the use of the terminals as well as the smartphones that patrons will be paying with.

Participate in Google Offers

Google Offers is Google's location promotion service. Visit http://www .google.com/offers/business to participate in Google Offers, and contact Google at this separate link, https://services.google.com/fb/forms/google offerscontact, to participate in Google's new Google Offers program and to tie it to Google Wallet.

NFC and PayPal for Mobile Payments

Use NFC through PayPal to facilitate mobile payments at your library. You can do this with the PayPal and Bump partnership, wherein PayPal makes it possible to make mobile payments using the popular Bump application for tapping phones together (see Figure 5.23).

You can also use the PayPal Mobile application. The PayPal Mobile app for Android devices allows users to transfer money by entering the amount and tapping their phones or waving them nearby and then entering their PIN.

Another option for leveraging mobile payments with PayPal is to offer your own customized mobile payment product. Create a mobile application to collect mobile payments with PayPal for your library with Titanium+ Commerce (http://www.appcelerator.com/products/titaniumcommerce/).

▶ Figure 5.23: PayPal NFC

Using Non-NFC Technologies to Collect Mobile Payments

Use Square as a mobile point-of-sale device to free library payments from the circulation desk. Square is a product that allows you to accept credit card payments with your iPhone, iPad, or Google Android smartphones. Unlike Google Wallet, with Square you can read real credit cards, not their virtual component. Square provides an external accessory that reads the card swipes and feeds the information into a mobile application on the device. Acquire a free Square card reader from an Apple store or online from Square (https://squareup.com/).

Use NFC at Your Library beyond Mobile Payments

With NFC-enabled smart posters you can turn advertisements into interactive points of access. Add NFC tags to posters so patrons can get more information just by waving or tapping their phone. This brings advanced interaction well beyond the library. Create library marketing flyers that include NFC tags with library contact info so that patrons can get the number and call the library just by waving their phone at the flyer.

NFC can also be used for uploading files, such as pictures to group digital displays, and sharing files, such as class readings, syllabi, and notes. Use NFC to allow patrons to unlock study rooms, workstations, lockers, and carrels. Enable your public printers with NFC technology so that patrons can print simply by tapping their phone against the printer.

Add NFC to location-based networking at your library by creating NFC tags that patrons can scan to check in to Foursquare. Share your library's reference business card with your patrons' mobile device with NFC. Patron information may soon be able to be associated with patrons' smartphones, allowing checkouts and more through NFC.

▶ 6

MARKETING

- ▶ Market Your Library's Foursquare Projects
- ▶ Use Gowalla
- ▶ Market Your Library's Use of Facebook Places
- ▶ Market Your Library's QR Code Campaign
- ▶ Market Your Library's Augmented Reality Endeavors
- ▶ Market Your Library's Instagram Programs

Marketing is essential, even for the most obviously beneficial programs. Nothing can sell itself if no one is aware of it. Market the projects to make sure that potential users are aware of the service and its benefits to them. Advertise the value of the library's presence in and engagement with these technologies.

Many services engaging location-aware technologies will promote themselves to the select patron groups already active with the tools. They market themselves and the library in their own ways, within their internal communities and through the natural reach they provide. Maximize the discoverability of your physical library within the location-based elements of these mobile/social technologies. Put it on the map.

However, most projects should be marketed within and beyond the technologies themselves to bolster awareness and ensure success in meeting their visibility among our patrons.

Places to Market These Services

- ▶ Within the technologies' communities
- ▶ Within the library itself, its physical surfaces
- ▶ Beyond the library, on campus bulletin boards, in cafés, at bus stops
- ▶ Online
- ▶ With social media
- ▶ With traditional media
- ▶ In person

▶ MARKET YOUR LIBRARY'S FOURSQUARE PROJECTS

Market your library's Foursquare projects with Foursquare and other location-based services, with social networks, with QR codes, and in your library.

Foursquare users will come across your library's venue within the network, so in a way its presence is its advertisement. Actively market your library's Foursquare programs with Foursquare promotions. Optimize your library's Foursquare location for discoverability.

Market your Foursquare initiative within Foursquare by optimizing the metadata of your library's Foursquare venue. Make sure its name (as known by visitors and possibly including parent institution and contact information) is correct and fully filled out, and assign a category and tags. Also make use of all Foursquare features as a user, including Tips, To Dos, and a Like It on Facebook button. Make sure the venue's location is accurate in the written address as well as on the visual map. Create specials to unlock this powerful feature meant for the purpose of marketing the Foursquare venue. Take advantage of the promotional decal provided by Foursquare when you claim the venue (see Figure 6.1).

Use Twitter to amplify the reach of your promotional efforts, create a dialog about your library's Foursquare presence, and invite engagement. Tweet to

▶ Figure 6.1: Market with the Foursquare Decal

announce specials, to share check-ins on FourSquare, to advertise links to and the name of the library's venue, and to promote competition for the mayorship and other rewards. Also use Instagram to post images of your venue's page, specials and prizes, and mayors.

Market your library's Foursquare presence in the library itself with signs advertising the Foursquare specials you create, with flyers that promote checking in while in the library to compete for points, and with QR codes posted around the library that link to the venue's page. Use digital signage to show recent check-ins, who is mayor, stats, and the dashboard. Use print ads to promote specials and motivate users to pursue mayorships.

Advertise Foursquare programs in person at the reference and other service desks as well as during instruction and orientation sessions. Mentioning that your library participates in Foursquare can often be enough to drive interest. Giving patrons a chance to use their mobile devices during the session is a great way to create a positive experience.

Advertise online as well with links to the venue on your site and QR codes with the venue's name and URL. Focus online marketing on Foursquare specials, and use brand with the Foursquare logo.

Market on your library's Facebook page in status updates, with links on your library's Facebook page as a posted picture and with other features, including Discussions and Notes. Maximize this venue by socially engaging your Facebook connections with Questions asking for prize suggestions and ways they might enjoy challenges.

▶USE GOWALLA

Use pictures within Gowalla, Gowalla Trips, and digital signage to market your Gowalla projects. Advertise your Gowalla presence through other location-based services such as with tips on your library's Foursquare venue page. Market your Gowalla campaign by securing branded icons and with your library's Twitter and Facebook programs by sending check-ins and links to the pages and as tweets.

▶MARKET YOUR LIBRARY'S USE OF FACEBOOK PLACES

Market your library's use of Facebook Places within Places by optimizing its page information, setting up successful Facebook Deals, with QR codes linking to your library's Places page, and with codes that directly check in visitors. Use your Facebook page to drive interaction about check-ins with Places, and encourage patrons to send their check-ins to their social graph and share the deals they gained.

The best way to market your library's Facebook Places venue is with Facebook. Optimize your presence within Facebook Places by claiming the venue, giving it a short but clear name and description, adding full data to the venue's page, and creating rewarding Facebook Deals on your library's Facebook page. Promote checking in to the library on Facebook Places with tweets that announce Facebook Deals and on the library website with links directly to your Places site.

Create QR codes that link to the mobile webpage for your library's Facebook Places venue with a caption encouraging check-ins. Post QR codes within your library that check in to Facebook Places for the patron or that simply announce it with text reading "check in to the Free Library on Facebook Places." Also use Instagram to promote Facebook Places by posting a picture that illustrates how to find and check in to the library on Places.

Market your library's Facebook Deals with flyers in the library, in advertisements in community newsletters, and on your library website. Craft deals in such a way as to best cater to patron interests, and advertise on the physical bulletin boards of local bookstores.

▶ MARKET YOUR LIBRARY'S QR CODE CAMPAIGN

Market your QR code campaigns in these ways:

- ▶ In the library, display art-like QR code posters, desk signs, window decals, and digital signage and distribute flyers.
- ▶ Online, share the QR codes digitally in subject guides, contact information pages, collections links, and information pages. Use them as featured images in page banners.
- ▶ Use QR codes in e-mail signatures (see Figure 6.2) and business cards.
- ▶ Post QR codes across social networks.
- ▶ Explain what a QR code is only once per medium.

QR codes tend to market themselves when visible in the library. They are eye catching, have visual appeal as both art and technology, and engender curiosity. They are still new enough to draw attention, immediately serving as a point of interest. Place a few QR codes prominently to attract attention and drive interest. Maximize this by posting them as you would post featured art and with attention-grabbing captions that play to the scanners' intrigue. Then post other functional QR codes in their relevant spaces in smaller sizes and more out of the way. Post QR codes in a fashion to meet patrons' expectations for displayed artwork, not just as flyers (which we are trained to ignore) and in unexpected areas. Also post codes exactly where patrons will expect to

▶ Figure 6.2: Market QR Codes in E-mail Signatures

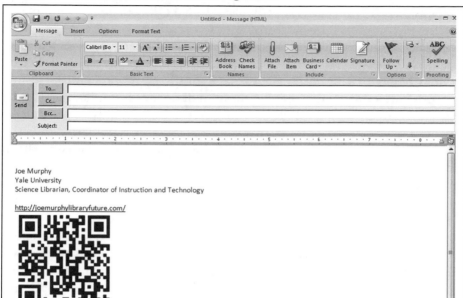

find informational flyers, grabbing their attention when they see the QR code instead of a text-based flyer.

Post QR codes beyond the library. Color and brand the QR codes to bring attention to and market your QR code campaign out in your community. They will stand out among the traditional flyers and bring links to the physical surrounding community. Include recognizable images, such as book or library icons, to draw the connection for passersby. Attach small QR codes to newsletters and flyers for existing marketing campaigns to subtly promote your library's use of codes. Include a caption or heading mentioning your library to associate the library's brand with this new technology. Use QR codes outside the library for topics that will have an interest with diffuse patrons. Codes can advertise events, link to popular online resources and reserves, and provide directions to or tips for the library.

Add QR codes to your library's homepage to draw wide attention to your project. QR codes posted on your webpage can include contact information for departments and library staff in contact file format, links to popular resources or e-books, upcoming events, and directions to tie their promotion directly to a practical value. Post a QR code that links to your library's location on Google maps. Post QR codes that link to mobile versions of your site, recommended resources, and calendar files of upcoming events.

Use online social networks to market your library's QR codes. Post QR codes as pictures on your Facebook page. Post a QR code for the library as a profile picture to garner a lot of quick attention. Use a QR code that includes a link to your library's webpage for this. Include short explanatory captions to market the codes as well as the programs they are part of. Create a folder of pictures in your Facebook page for the event, program, or service the codes are enhancing alongside traditional images from that same topic. Use Twitter by posting QR codes to third-party image applications including TwitPic and yfrog.

Of course, post QR codes to image-sharing social networks such as Flickr, Picasso, Instagram, Path, and picplz. Instagram is the perfect online venue for posting QR codes because it is an established community for sharing visual resources. Post as image files, and include appropriate metadata. Post with a concise caption that intrigues more than it explains. Associate the posted codes with a location and hashtags as appropriate. Post the QR codes you create for specific campaigns with short captions simply explaining what they are part of, or post a QR code to announce the program with a simple title promoting the technology, such as "QR codes connect the 3D world with rich online information," or "The library is using QR codes to add links to the real world."

▶ MARKET YOUR LIBRARY'S AUGMENTED REALITY ENDEAVORS

Market your library's augmented reality programs within the library with signs and with augmented reality tags posted with captions about what it will reveal. Market on Twitter and other online venues that hidden information can be displayed in the library, and post snapshots that give a glimpse of what information can be uncovered with augmented reality.

▶ MARKET YOUR LIBRARY'S INSTAGRAM PROGRAMS

Instagram has a strong internal community that is steadily growing, but that community can be too limited for self-promotion. Optimize your use of Instagram to maximize your library's impact. Fill out the optional Instagram user profile, attach a location to all posts, use hashtags whenever appropriate (but never overuse), and use a clear and unique profile icon. Engage your community to expand your audience by following relevant and potentially interested users within Instagram. Find contacts through your library's Twitter and Facebook accounts. Discover other patrons by seeing who has uploaded images at your library's location. Find relevant Instagram users by searching hashtags of topics on local interest.

Bring attention to your Instagram content well beyond the network by tying your Instagram account to your library's Twitter, Foursquare, Tumblr, and Facebook accounts within your Instagram account settings. Send pictures to Foursquare when posting images to Instagram to check in. Send picture uploads from Instagram to Twitter as a way of expanding the potential viewers. This advertises the images and your Instagram account. Make sure to always include an explanatory but catchy title, because posts sent to Twitter will appear only as links.

Images sent from Instagram to Facebook will also appear as links, so maximize the title text that will accompany them. Images shared to Facebook will function as links with a preview image, so make a comment about the image that includes an intriguing caption or poses a question that will create conversation. Instagram pictures sent to Facebook will function as visual moments around which to interact, so choose visual content that will create opportunities for timely discussion. These can include pictures of flyers for events and new books.

Use Instagram's filters to create unique images. Instagram's filters never fail to grab attention and are becoming famous as well as identifiable. Sharing Instagram pictures beyond the network is a great way to make use of their original appearance.

Bring Instagram posts to the physical world as well. Print Instagram images taken of your library, taken by accounts that are relevant to your library, or that feature a topic of timely relevance; use Instaprint or a similar service, and then post the pictures within your library on walls or in displays to draw a connection between the physical library and the online medium.

Include links to your Instagram account and individual images within social media profiles. Also link to RSS feeds from your Instagram account, as well as to particular images or links for searches in Instagram to interesting topics. Include your library's Instagram username in promotional venues: business cards, online profiles, within other image-sharing services, and as part of contact information on your website.

▶7

BEST PRACTICES

- ▶ Organize Your Best Practices
- ▶ Prioritize Your Practical Considerations
- ▶ Train Your Staff
- ▶ Assign Work Flow Appropriately

▶ORGANIZE YOUR BEST PRACTICES

Best practices and practical considerations are the important detail areas that make the success of projects with location-aware technologies. Outlining detailed best practices for implementing such technology programs can be time-consuming, but attention paid to details at the beginning can ensure success for the project's long term. Be comprehensive, and include these best practices:

- ▶ Plan for and meeting practical considerations.
- ▶ Balance real-world complications with philosophical priorities.
- ▶ Train staff for awareness of and familiarity with all aspects of the projects.
- ▶ Prepare staff for familiarity with the technology areas.
- ▶ Maximize usability of the technologies.
- ▶ Inform projects from the angle of technology users:
  - ➤ Create accounts within location-based services versus using staff accounts.
  - ➤ Use naming conventions that align closer to how people expect to discover venue titles and that balance the formal titles we have for our libraries.
- ▶ Use the appropriate amount of signage to avoid overkill for QR codes, considering the larger areas and local communities we fit in.
- ▶ Consider branding when creating QR codes to help your codes stand out by adding colors or logos versus the level of the code's successful scanability.

► Combine projects, such as Foursquare and Instagram.
► Insert your library's location strategy into your larger social media and mobile strategies.
► Think about these technologies beyond service enhancements as other areas such as publishing also change to adapt to them.
► Engage these technologies from a standpoint of opportunities to teach your patrons about the tools.

► PRIORITIZE YOUR PRACTICAL CONSIDERATIONS

As when you organize your best practices, be comprehensive when you prioritize your practical considerations. Be sure to account for:

► management concerns,
► management solutions,
► potential costs,
► staff training,
► work flows for implementing programs with location-based services,
► steps for creating QR codes,
► responsibility for posting and editing QR codes,
► staff duties for creating and advertising augmented reality programs,
► sustainability of the projects, and
► project scalability.

Most of the technologies discussed in this book are free to use, but none of them are zero cost because each entails a level of cost in staff time, training, and upkeep. A very few may require monetary costs, for example, to print QR codes and customize icon Stamps for Gowalla.

Staff considerations for applying augmented reality will focus on promoting staff awareness of the technology and its usage, seeking staff input, marketing, testing, and planning for continuity and change. Also addressed should be training for reference librarians as an information resource and training for staff as frontline device providers.

Each of the technology projects discussed in this book represents a change in the form of an addition to the services library staff are used to providing, tools they are used to using, and service models that may differ greatly from traditional ones. Such changes cause stress, so include a plan to help manage staff stress. Managers and trainers should ease and not push adoption of the technologies and projects. Show that staff will be supported through the change, while demonstrating that deconstructive resistance is not an option.

Supporting and making the change happen is a major management consideration. Consider what other library activities to give up as you add a service possibly without additional staff resources. Consider that changes in the technologies, as well as changes you may make to adapt the projects to assessment findings, may impact details about the programs, so design strategies for supporting the services with plans for shifting or cancelling pilots.

Understand and address the potential privacy concerns for patrons when possibly encountering and managing access to their private data. Plan for addressing privacy concerns for staff engaging in the tools, and prepare to answer questions about privacy implications regarding the technology itself.

▶TRAIN YOUR STAFF

Staff members need to be provided training for these projects in order to gain their support for the programs, enable them to speak about the goals to patrons and possibly media, and ensure the cohesive success of the program. Considerations and practical questions for staff training include:

- ▶ planning for training time and resources,
- ▶ articulating the need for training,
- ▶ deciding who in the library needs to be provided with training,
- ▶ identifying who will provide the training,
- ▶ deciding what skills the training will cover,
- ▶ determining the exact content of the training so that staff gain a familiarity with the technologies, and
- ▶ planning when the training will be repeated and updated.

All staff, even those not involved in creating or supporting the technology of the project directly, should be included in training. This will create a cohesive, supportive environment for the projects. All staff should be fully versed in the technology and its uses, the goals of the project, and how patrons can engage with the technology in case staff are called on to answer questions about the program by patrons, the media, or even fellow staff or outside colleagues. Technical staff may be called on to help with online aspects of the project, and administrators need to understand the goals and considerations.

Training for any staff interacting with the project directly should include full familiarity with the technology from the perspective of the tool's users. Staff have to use the tool in real situations in order to fully understand its benefits. For example, staff should know how to scan and create QR codes, why and how to use Foursquare, how to claim a Facebook Deal with Facebook Places, and how to add a location to an Instagram post. Staff should also be familiar with the philosophical side of using the technologies, including why people like to share their location, what the potential privacy concerns may be, what the expectations for sharing or oversharing are, and how users of the technology expect to engage with a location.

Training staff that will be running a Foursquare program for your library should include:

- ▶ how to create a venue,
- ▶ how to track statistics,
- ▶ how to add a Tip,
- ▶ how to claim a venue,
- ▶ how to create specials, and
- ▶ how specials will be rewarded.

Training for staff running your library's Facebook Places should include how to claim the library's Facebook Places venue, how to create a Deal, and how to provide rewards for patrons claiming deals.

Training staff who are creating QR codes should include an overview of how the codes will be scanned and used. They should be taught the various options for creating QR codes, how to evaluate QR code generators, how to choose a size for the codes generated, how to export and save the files of the codes, how and where to store the code files, and what type of code to use (hyperlink, contact file, calendar file, etc.). Staff should be trained in applying the codes to flyers, webpages, e-mail signatures, posters, and business cards in various file types. Staff completing technical steps for the project should also be given a complete overview and understanding of the steps in engaging the codes before and after the stage of their contribution.

Training should be done in a loose, relaxed, nonthreatening environment where staff can engage in play and experiment with the tools in order to gain a personal level of familiarity. Staff familiar with the technologies leading the project should coordinate training initiatives in conjunction with support materials from relevant companies that make the technology products. Dedicated teams of staff with advanced experience can serve as training supports. Training opportunities can combine in-person, asynchronous, and virtual components. Include example projects that focus on gaining experience in technical steps. Training can include scheduled repeated sessions to provide learning opportunities throughout the process. Ongoing training can also serve as opportunities to update the skills needed as the technologies change and the projects evolve.

So that non-mobile-literate staff will become familiar with such devices, provide opportunities for these staff to directly engage the technology through mobile devices. Mobile literacy can also set the framework to help staff understand the value and roles of these technologies and thus help with staff buy-in. Provide a smartphone or tablet through your institution if possible; if not, solicit staff to volunteer sharing their devices. Have the staff try each activity that makes up usage of the technology. Provide opportunities for staff to try the technologies beyond the library within their own lives if possible.

▶ ASSIGN WORK FLOW APPROPRIATELY

Work flows for designing and maintaining services that leverage location-based services need to address who is responsible for each stage, including:

- ▶ claiming venues,
- ▶ creating promotions,
- ▶ adding metadata to venue pages,
- ▶ interacting with patrons,
- ▶ working with patrons to claim their rewards,
- ▶ tracking statistics, and
- ▶ marketing promotions.

Work flows should also specify how schedules of responsibility for duties are allocated and who will do what and when to ensure timely service and to avoid overlap.

Staff work flows and practices for creating and posting QR codes can easily be dominated by lead staff with clear articulation of how other staff will contribute to the multiple public aspects of the project. Work flows for QR code campaigns cover who generates the codes, how and where they are exported and saved, who will convert the saved files into posted formats, including signs, and who will post the flyers and test their attached QR codes. Continuity across staff changes and code needs should be accounted for, and time for staff to dedicate for the project needs to be formally secured.

▶8

METRICS

▶ Apply Metrics to Your Project

▶ Track Metrics for Patron Engagement

▶APPLY METRICS TO YOUR PROJECT

Applying metrics is essential for evaluating the success of location-aware technology projects. The statistics they generate help us gauge our approaches to the programs, assess our methods, and plan for future steps. Some general applications of metrics from usage of these services include:

▶ measuring the success of your Foursquare promotional specials,
▶ comparing various location-based service applications against each other,
▶ determining the most popular places for posting QR codes,
▶ measuring the success of and revising your augmented reality campaign, and
▶ assessing the success of Facebook Deals.

It is relatively easy to apply metrics to most location-aware technologies. Some examples of items to focus your metrics on for these tools include:

▶ Foursquare check-in numbers at your library;
▶ Foursquare Tips and To Dos that have been added by patrons;
▶ check-in statistics for your library, including demographics, times, and sharing;
▶ points earned by patrons on your library's Gowalla leaderboard;
▶ number of check-ins at your library's Facebook Places page;
▶ Likes and comments on your Instagram posts;
▶ number of photographs posted to Instagram at your library;
▶ scans and clicks on URLs in QR codes; and
▶ completed tasks initiated by QR codes in your library.

You can easily watch statistics for your library's Foursquare venue by logging in and looking at your library venue's dashboard if you have claimed the venue as manager. View venue statistics for the past day, week, 30 days, or 60 days. See the average number of check-ins per day over that time period. See which patron has the most check-ins of all time and how many times he or she has visited. Track general demographics of your visitors, including gender and age range. See the most recent visitors who have checked in and the brief information about those patrons that they have associated with their Foursquare account.

You can even track quite a few statistics without claiming your library's Foursquare venue. Anyone can view the number of check-ins, tips left, and visitors at a particular Foursquare venue. You can also view who the mayor is without claiming the venue, which may be helpful for running unofficial promotional campaigns (see Figure 8.1).

Use daily or weekly Foursquare check-ins to supplement gate counts measuring physical visitors to the library. Incentivize visits to the library and encourage check-ins as a way to measure how well the promotion works.

Use Foursquare's new Lists feature to measure and expand the impact of your library's Foursquare presence. Watch how many Foursquare users have added your library to their lists or follow the lists that you create. Watch how many people follow the list from within Foursquare. Invite your patrons to contribute to the lists and assess the level of interaction and collaboration that this generates.

▶ Figure 8.1: Monitor Foursquare Venue Usage Statistics

▶TRACK METRICS FOR PATRON ENGAGEMENT

Track metrics for patron engagement of your library through Gowalla by watching how many people check in to the venue, how many times they have checked in, how many highlights they have added, and how many photos they have added. Watch recent check-ins online or through the Gowalla mobile application. Track the number of users who complete Gowalla Trips created by your library and the number of trips that include your library.

Measure the reach of your library's use of the photo-sharing application Instagram by tracking the number of Likes that the photos you post to Instagram receive individually and in total. Also watch the number and quality of comments left on your Instagram photos. Tabulate these interactions weekly. Qualify the conversations and value added by conversations via comments. Keep watch on how many photos are taken and uploaded within Instagram at your library by checking the library's location within the app or online. Measure clicks on custom short links posted within titles, comments, and images by tracking their statistics through link tracking tools like Bitly. Track clicks from scans of QR code images you post to Instagram by assigning and tracking unique URLs created through bit.ly or Google's URL shortening service. Also watch for pictures of your library taken with Instagram and sent to Twitter, Facebook, and Tumblr. This expansion from Instagram outward multiplies the social reach of your library. Watch for this in Facebook by scanning current picture feeds of your Facebook contacts in the "Most Recent" Facebook tab.

Easily gather metrics for your QR code campaign by tracking clicks on links within QR codes through Bitly (see Figure 8.2). Use these metrics to measure and make decisions about services, including reference service desks, collection areas, display spaces, and specific resources. Use Google Analytics to watch traffic coming into specified webpages linked to with your QR codes. Track which codes posted in which locations are scanned more by tracking clicks on their unique links. Use this data to determine which locations are best for posting QR codes. Also combine this data with foot traffic patterns to gauge the impact of posted codes in each location on the flow of patrons through that area. You can also use visual cues such as observing patrons scanning and using QR codes in your library.

Track the usage of associated online content by watching web traffic to those resources with usage statistics as well as by measuring the use of those resources through citations. Watch the impact on attached services: increase in text messages sent to the reference phone, registrations on mobile-friendly sign-up sheets, direct downloads of digital content, and so forth.

▶ Figure 8.2: Track QR Code Activity with Bitly

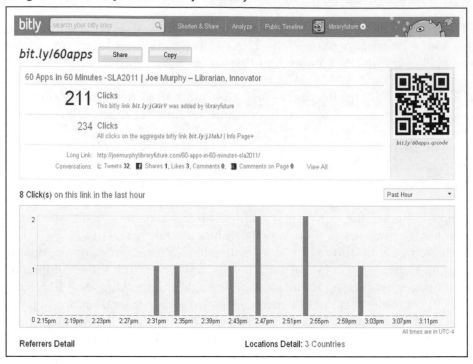

You can track statistics for your library's Facebook Places by watching the number of patrons who check in using it at your library. Check at any time how many patrons check in to your library using Facebook Places by watching the counter on the left-hand screen of the library's Facebook site. Also track how many people are checking in to the Facebook page, not just Places, for your library by watching the same counter on this page.

Another metric to note is the level of engagement these check-ins lead to on the library's Places page or Facebook page and the number of check-in posts and check-ins at your library that your patrons share in their Facebook streams. Also track related activities, such as posts or pictures added to your library's Places page as well as comments on posts and pictures. You can also watch which of your Facebook friends are checking in nearby with the Facebook mobile app "Map" feature within the Places tab. This can be useful in identifying how many of your Facebook connections are using Places.

Track how many patrons claim your library's Facebook Deals and how many they claimed. Track the demographics of patrons who claim your Facebook Deals and which are most successful. Statistics for Deals claimed can be tracked by staff awarding the Deals at service points. Make sure to instruct staff in how to track the deals claimed and what information they should collect from the patron.

Measure how much your library's reach has been extended with your augmented reality programs. Track usage of library-created layers in Layar and clicks on links to recommended augmented reality layers or services. Track engagement with services and programs from augmented reality applications by creating custom paths for patrons through these avenues.

Track metrics for your library on Bizzy. See how many people have Checked Out at your library using Bizzy, what they said if they commented in their checkout, and how they rated your library.

Use of some services, like Alfred, may be more difficult to measure. One suggestion is to promote the use of Alfred by patrons by rewarding those who can prove that they have placed your library's venue within the app. This method provides for an opportunity to simultaneously gauge and measure patron use.

Klout.com, the online social media metrics tracking service, has recently added several location-aware products to the suite of services it tracks, including Foursquare and Instagram. Use Klout to measure and report on some of your social metrics and to gauge potential influencers among your end users to target for promotions.

►9

DEVELOPING TRENDS

- ► Watch for New Services
- ► Expect Augmented Reality Technology to Expand
- ► Anticipate New Services Based on New Partnerships

Change is a consistent element of mobile technology trends, and the state of location-aware technology is a constantly moving target. There have been many developments in this field just during the writing of this book; sections had to be added, removed, and rewritten to make sure the content was as current as possible. There will still be technologies discussed in this book that may no longer be around or that have been totally transformed by the time it is published. There are services that will emerge and become popular between the writing and reading of this book. In this section I will outline the next emerging trends in this technology space and some of the foreseeable near-future developments. I will share my predictions and will try to gauge the predominant trend areas that will guide upcoming directions.

►WATCH FOR NEW SERVICES

The major areas of developing trends for location-aware technologies are:

- ► micro local flash deals,
- ► the addition of location elements to entertainment check-ins,
- ► more local group buying,
- ► location-based services changing to be more like local discovery tools,
- ► more user input opportunities provided within location check-in services,
- ► the spread of QR codes to wider user groups,
- ► the extension of QR codes to deeper applications, and
- ► the introduction of near field communication to services.

Foursquare will likely expand beyond the location activity check-in and into local exploration and social discovery, and Facebook Places will continue its trajectory into direct engagement between brands and customers. Loopt unveiled a new service, Loopt Qs, which allows users to ask and answer questions about a location. It is used to solicit feedback or share information about a venue.

The future for QR codes will be one of growth. More and more industries will pick up the use of QR codes, mutually fueling their growth across user segments. As awareness and usage of QR codes spreads, so too will institutions' willingness to apply them to a wider swatch of services.

Future applications of QR codes for libraries may include deeper, more powerful applications, performing such functions as exporting citations of specific items, checking out a book to a patron just by scanning it, casting votes, or supplying feedback. Future QR codes may provide direct access to electronic content. These can initiate direct downloads of specific e-books or launch streaming access to designated cloud content. If library content is linked to cloud reading services, those already in existence and those being developed soon, QR codes might be used to connect patrons to content such as downloadable e-books and articles without the library otherwise serving as a middle partner.

Cloud reading applications and access to electronic content not downloaded to patrons' devices may soon have location-specific or location-sensitive elements. Access to content with cloud reading services may use proximity-based authentication, and the location of a reader may soon be an element of content discovery or ranked relevance.

Near field communication is a growing technology that allows mobile devices to exchange information with other devices in very close proximity by touching or by using special tags. Though not entirely new, near field communication is rapidly expanding into new service areas, including making payments. Near field communication tags can also provide functions similar to QR codes by providing information or links. Google's use of near field communication for its recently released mobile payment system will help to bring the technology to the masses (see Figure 9.1).

One of the biggest trends in location-aware mobile technology this year is mobile payments. Services for using mobile devices as supplements to making and receiving payments are expanding. One company, Square, provides a small device to attach to your iPhone or iPad that reads credit cards and a mobile application for processing payments made in person. Square makes the smartphone or tablet itself a mobile point-of-sale tool. Libraries can apply this service to circulation operations, using it to collect fees from anywhere, freeing the staff from the cash register behind the desk. The practical considerations for adopting such technologies will include new operations skills and work flows, an acceptance of the mobile device as part

▶ Figure 9.1: Google Wallet PayPass Payment Processor

of the work infrastructure, and a shift in the philosophy of where and how library services can be provided.

▶ EXPECT AUGMENTED REALITY TECHNOLOGY TO EXPAND

The next developments in augmented reality will be a slow but steady growth in awareness of the technology by expanded visibility of major services. The continued growth of smartphones will assist with the extension of the technology's acceptance across user groups. The applications of augmented reality will soon expand into recognition of text and people, supplying visible layers of information to our experience within content and with service representatives.

Augmented reality has the best years of its life ahead of it. The future of augmented reality will be expansion into new markets and industries—any service, product, or presence with a real-world element that can be enhanced by additional digital information. Augmented reality can only grow from here. The possible roles for libraries within the world of augmented reality are also ones that can only grow:

▶ The library will expand beyond the shelves and into locations where information is experienced.
▶ The near future of libraries and augmented reality is providing seamless access to online resources to established augmented reality products so that the rich information resources we have to offer can be part of our patrons' information experience in their shifting real-world access points.

▶ More focus will be placed on serving as purveyors of location contextual information.

▶ There will be more access to resources to places and not only portals.

▶ There will be a larger focus on the skills needed by our patrons to effectively engage in information in these venues.

▶ The partnership between libraries as resource providers and augmented reality product developers will deepen. Libraries will also begin to develop more augmented reality programs of their own, designing and supporting the services.

▶ As libraries engage augmented reality, more and more library staff will have to gain more skills to ensure their libraries' success in these realms and their own continued relevance within the information industry.

▶ANTICIPATE NEW SERVICES BASED ON NEW PARTNERSHIPS

Group buying services including Groupon and Living Social will likely continue their impressive growth as the idea of locally relevant discounts combined with social collaboration takes root in our everyday experience. We will see more partnerships between group buying and other location-aware technologies, such as the recent team-up between Groupon and Loopt wherein Loopt will send you notifications when you are near a Groupon instant flash deal (see Figure 9.2). This may well expand into areas of library services, including patron-driven acquisition and securing and making decisions on library and community spaces.

Another quickly emerging trend area to take note of is that of local flash deals. These services create local deals or promotions for your place that have hyper time sensitivity to attract passersby or drive traffic at specific times. These leverage the idea of moment- and space-specific relevancy for advertising and creating interest to drive engagement.

Mobile photo-sharing applications will continue to expand in numbers of members and of applications. More and more location-relevant services will add image elements as well as make use of the existing community and photo resources of services such as Instagram and picplz. Instagram will partner with more content brands, and services will apply the visual stories from Instagram to their on-site experience. The future of the location-heavy mobile photo-sharing application Color will be interesting to watch as an example of possible next waves in social/photo engagement based on proximity. It may continue to blaze a trail that guides other developments, or it may develop in areas more acceptable to current expectations.

Ultimately, the biggest trend will be the expanding penetration of location as a point of interaction and access to more areas of emerging technologies and

▶ Figure 9.2: Loopt Notification of a Nearby Groupon Deal

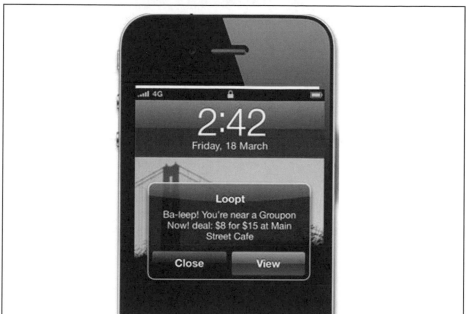

our networked behaviors. Location is entering many layers of our information experience, and libraries have a wide role to play in this trend.

Location-based technologies are always under rapid evolution. New products are emerging and services are refined and remade. At the end of 2011, Oink and Pinterest were introduced with wide success, Gowalla was bought by Facebook, and Foursquare added its Lists and Radar features. See the companion website (http://www.alatechsource.org/techset/) for up-to-date information on emerging trends.

▶

RECOMMENDED READING

The field of location-based technology is always changing and very quickly, so these recommended reading resources focus on current awareness. This collection of websites, blogs, Twitter feeds, presentations, and papers will help you stay on top of this dynamic field, covering the practical knowledge and analysis needed for success with this technology.

▶TECHNOLOGY NEWS OUTLETS

Start with current technology news outlets, such as http://mashable.com/ and http://techcrunch.com/. Maximize Mashable by making use of its Follow feature (http://mashable.com/follow/) to follow stories on such topics as these:

- ▶ Location at http://mashable.com/follow/topics/location
- ▶ Foursquare at http://mashable.com/follow/topics/foursquare
- ▶ Gowalla at http://mashable.com/follow/topics/gowalla
- ▶ Loopt at http://mashable.com/follow/topics/loopt
- ▶ GeoLocation at http://mashable.com/follow/topics/geolocation

Use social media channels to fit these news streams into your life flow:

- ▶ http://www.facebook.com/mashable
- ▶ http://twitter.com/#!/mashable
- ▶ http://www.facebook.com/techcrunch
- ▶ http://twitter.com/#!/techcrunch

▶BLOGS AND TWITTER FEEDS

Follow the blogs of products and companies in the center of this technology at http://blog.foursquare.com/.

Watch what Marissa Mayer, Vice President of Location and Local Services at Google, is saying at http://twitter.com/#!/marissamayer.

See Eric Gordon's blog at http://placeofsocialmedia.com/blog/index .php. Eric also has a book available on this topic: Gordon, Eric, and Adriana de Souza e Silva. 2011. *Net Locality: Why Location Matters in a Networked World.* Hoboken, NJ: Wiley-Blackwell.

► ONLINE PRESENTATIONS

Online presentations are another great way to learn more about these technologies and their applications. Some of my previous presentations on this topic are available on SlideShare:

- ► "Location Aware Technology & Libraries." Keynote. February 16, 2011. http://www.slideshare.net/joseph.murphy/keynote-location-based-tech.
- ► "Mayor of the Library: Foursquare & Location-Based Mobile Social Networks." May 12, 2010. http://www.slideshare.net/joseph.murphy/ mayor-of-the-library.
- ► "Check in at the Future of Libraries." June 8, 2010. http://www .slideshare.net/joseph.murphy/checkinfuture.
- ► "Check in w/ Location Based Mobile Services: Foursquare and Libraries." July 20, 2010. http://www.slideshare.net/joseph.murphy/ lbs-acrl-murphy.

Fellow librarians have also produced great presentations, such as "Beyond Foursquare: Library Treks with SCVNGR" at http://www.slideshare.net/ joseph.murphy/cil11-hhlib-preconf-amy-v-beyond-four-square-mellinger- vecchione.

► AWARENESS TOOLS

Leverage Facebook as a current awareness tool by Liking relevant Facebook Pages, including product pages such as the following. These are great because they tend to address topics related to the larger field of location awareness and not only their products:

- ► Foursquare at http://www.facebook.com/foursquare
- ► Gowalla at http://www.facebook.com/gowalla
- ► Loopt at http://www.facebook.com/Loopt
- ► Bizzy at http://www.facebook.com/BizzyFans
- ► Foodspotting at http://www.facebook.com/Foodspotting
- ► Booyah at http://www.facebook.com/BooyahFans

INDEX

Page numbers followed by the letter "f" indicate figures.

A

Accelerometer, 11, 48
Account, creating, 21–23, 30–31
Alfred account, 71–73, 72f, 99
Allard Pierson Museum, 48
Analytics, 13, 40, 40f–41f, 95, 97–100
    See also Metrics
Android
    devices, 57–58
    digital wallet, 76–79, 79f
    Layar, 51–52
    location-aware services and, 1–5,
        2f–3f
    log-in, 14
    QR code, 57, 62
    Shelvar, 53–54
API. *See* Application programming
    interface (API)
Apple.com
    App Store, 57
    iTunes, 14, 37, 49, 50
    Layar, 51–52
    location-aware services and, 1–5, 2f–3f
    marketplace, 14
    square card reader, 79, 79f
Application programming interface (API),
    67, 70–71
Architecture 3D, 51
ARSights, 48
Augmented reality
    accelerometer, 11
    applications, 14–15
    bar codes, two-dimensional, 4, 12–13,
        55, 57
    camera, 11
    custom content, 50–53, 51f
    defined, 11, 48
    examples, 12
    GPS chip, 11, 48
    information accessing, 4
    library and, 47–49, 49f, 50
    marketing, 86
    photo-sharing applications, 12
    program, 47–49
    QR code campaign, 55–58, 56f
    shelf reading and, 53–54, 53f
    strategic management, 21–23
    tags, 48
    trends, 103–104
    uses of, 54–55
    Virtual Graffiti, 15, 49–50, 49f

B

Badges, 10, 29, 38–40, 38f–39f
Bar codes, two-dimensional, 4, 12–13, 55,
    57
Barcode Scanner, 57
BeeTagg, 14, 57
Beluga, 16, 17f
Best practices
    organizing, 89–90
    prioritizing, 90–91
    staff training, 22–23, 26–27, 30, 47, 54,
        77–78, 90–93

Best practices *(cont'd.)*
  work flow, 93
  See also Marketing
Bitly, 14, 63, 97–98, 98f
Bizzy, 16, 20, 71, 73–75, 74f, 99
Blog, 55, 65, 70–71, 74
Book reviews, 60–61, 61f–62f
Bookmarks, 64–65
Booyah MyTown, 3, 16, 17f
Brainstorming, 23
Branding, 45, 63, 68, 89
Brands, 36, 38–40, 85
Brightkite, 16
Brinkman, Bo, 53

C
Catalog (OPAC). *See* Library catalog
  (OPAC)
Citi MasterCard, 76
Clever Sense, 72
Cloud, 57, 102
Color, 15, 85, 104

D
Darien (CT) Library, 36
Dashboard, 83, 95–96
Delivr.com code generator, 14, 61–62
Digital signage, 57, 60, 63, 83–84
Digital wallet, 75–79, 77f–79f, 101–103,
  103f
District of Columbia Public Library
  (DCPL), 2

E
E-mail, 13–14, 30, 35, 60–62, 65
E-mail signatures, 56–57, 65, 84–85, 85f, 92
Extragr.am map feature, 71

F
Facebook
  account, 3, 44
  Bizzy and, 73–74
  Deals, 43, 45–47, 95
  Gowalla, 64–65, 105
  hashtags, 68–70, 69f
  linking, 14, 58–59, 62–63
  location awareness, 1, 2f, 10, 71
  marketing, 74, 82–87

  monitoring, 95–96
  Pages vs. Places, 44–45
  patrons and, 42–44, 43f
  QR code, 13–14
  staff and, 90–93
  statistics, 40, 40f–41f
  tagging, 10
  themes and trends, 20–21, 101
  Wall, 35
Facebook Places
  application, 13
  Gowalla, 63–67, 66f, 83–86, 85f
  linking, 58–59, 62–63
  location-aware services, 1–5, 2f, 9, 11,
    13, 43f
  Map feature, 98–99
  marketing, 74, 83–84
  metrics, 95–98
  privacy and, 5, 27
Feedity.com, 71
Findability, 30, 68–69
Flickr, 68, 71, 86
Foodspotting, 20
Foursquare
  accounts, 21–23, 30–31
  application, 12
  attendance tracking, 42
  badges, 38–40, 38f–39f
  brands, 36, 38–40
  campaign, 29–33
  claim confirmation, 32–33, 33f
  Gowalla, 63–67, 66f, 83–86, 85f
  linking, 32, 62–63
  Lists feature, 105
  location information quality, 71
  location-aware services and, 1–5, 2f–3f,
    12
  marketing and, 33–36, 34f, 81–83, 82f,
    87
  mayorships, 10, 12, 29, 31, 33–36, 34f,
    62, 83, 96
  platform, 32, 35
  QR codes and, 62
  Radar feature, 105
  rewards, 11–12, 23, 29–30, 33–36, 33f,
    36–38
  staff and, 41–44, 43f, 90–93
  statistics, 40, 40f–41f, 95–96, 96f

strategic management, 21–23
themes and trends, 20–21, 102
tips, 37–38, 38f, 92
venue, 10, 14, 30–33, 31f, 33f, 35–39, 92

G

Geolocation, 3–4, 13, 52
GetGlue, 20
Google
    Analytics, 13, 97–99
    Goo.gl, 14, 63
    Latitude, 16
    Maps, 14, 58, 85
    Offers program, 75, 77–78
    Places, 16, 20, 52
    Prepaid Card, 76–77
    QR code, 14, 57, 63
    searching, 10
    URL shortening service, 97
    Wallet, 75–78, 77f, 79f, 102, 103f
Gowalla
    best practices, 90
    highlights, 13, 64, 66–67, 66f, 97
    implications of, 9–11
    location-aware services and, 1–5, 3f, 7
    marketing and, 63–67, 66f, 83–86, 85f
    metrics and, 95, 97
    rewards, 13, 67
    themes and trends, 20–21, 105
GPS, 4, 11, 48, 65
GroupMe, 16, 17f
Groupon, 20, 104, 105f

H

Hashtags, 15, 39, 52, 67–70, 69f, 86
Highlights, 13, 64, 66–67, 66f, 97
Hotmail, 65
HTML, QR code, 13, 57

I

Icons, 17f, 30, 38, 57, 63, 66, 83, 85–86, 90
Images, 15, 15f, 20, 44–45, 48, 52, 55,
        57–58, 66–69
    QR code, 7, 13, 83–87
    RSS feed, 70–71
Implementation. *See* Project management
InCrowd, 4, 16, 86–87
i-nigma, 14

Instagram
    best practices, 89–91
    filters, 87
    hashtags, 68–70, 69f
    location-based photo stream, 69–71
    managing, 71
    marketing, 83–84, 86–87
    photo sharing, 10, 12, 15, 15f, 20, 51,
        104
    statistics, 95, 97–99
iPhone, location-aware services and, 1–5,
        2f–3f
iTunes, 14, 37, 49, 50

K

Kaywa, QR code generator, 13, 61–62
Klout.com, 99

L

Layar, 12, 14–15, 48–49, 51–53, 51f, 99
Library
    book reviews, 60–61, 61f–62f
    Google Wallet, 75–78, 77f, 79f, 102, 103f
    location-awareness services, 5–8, 11
    management support, 25–28
    metrics and, 95–99
    patrons, 4, 46, 74–75, 99
    patrons, Gowalla and, 63–67, 66f, 83–86,
        85f
    shelving, 15, 53–54, 53f
    staff, 26–27, 59, 90–93
    statistics, 40, 40f–41f, 95, 97–99
    strategic management, 21–23
    trends, 103–104
    website, 84
Library catalog (OPAC), 59–60, 60f, 62–63
"Link Method," 26
LinkedIn, 14
Linking
    augmented reality, 49, 54
    Bizzy, 74
    bar codes, two-dimensional, 4, 12–13,
        55, 57
    catalog, 59–60
    Foursquare, 32
    Google, 78
    Gowalla, 64–65
    library, 52, 56–59, 102

Linking *(cont'd.)*
  location-based services, 62–63
  marketing, 68, 74, 83–84
  metrics, 97–99
  QR codes and, 55, 84–85
  social media, 14, 43–45, 58–59, 86
Living Social, 104
Local
  discovery tools, 101–102
  recommendations, 71–75, 72f, 74f,
      104–105, 105f
  user review service, 16
Location-awareness services
  advantages and disadvantages, 9–10
  applications, 1, 3–5, 2f–3f, 12–13, 15–17,
      16f–17f
  contact information, 4
  designing, 16–17, 17f
  Foursquare, 9–12, 17
  Layar, 14–16
  hashtags, 15, 39, 52, 67–70, 69f, 86
  implications, 9–11
  information quality, 71
  local user review, 71–75, 72f, 74f,
      101–102
  photo sharing, 12, 15f, 15, 67, 85, 104
  promotional, 33–34, 33f, 35–38, 38f,
      39–40, 39f, 81–83, 82f
  QR codes and, 1, 3–5, 2f–3f, 5–8,
      12–14
  strategic management, 21–23
  technologies, 11–14
  tools, 16–17, 16f–17f
  Twitter, 1, 4, 16, 20, 71
Logo, 83, 89
Loopt, 4, 16, 102, 105f

M
Marketing
  audience, 27–28, 29–33
  augmented reality and, 86–87
  Facebook Places, 83–84
  Foursquare, 33–34, 33f, 35–38, 38f,
      39–40, 39f, 81–83, 82f
  Gowalla and, 63–67, 66f, 83–86, 85f
  hashtags, 68–70, 69f
  Instagram programs, 86–87
  internal, 27–28

  prizes, 12, 23, 29–30, 33–36, 33f, 81–83,
      82f
  public demonstration, 27, 30
  QR codes campaign, 55–59, 56f, 58f,
      60–63, 60f–61f, 84–86, 85f
  social media, 74, 82–83, 86–87
  Twitter, 74, 82–83, 86–87
Mashable.com, 48, 62
Mayorships, 10, 12, 29, 31, 33–36, 34f, 62,
    83, 96
Metadata, 3, 16, 68, 71, 82, 86, 93
Metrics
  analytics, 97–99
  applying, 95–96, 96f
  Google Analytics, 13, 97–99
  monitoring, 95–96, 96f
  patron use, 97–99, 98f
  statistics, 40, 40f–41f, 95, 97–99
  tracking, 97–99
Miami University, 53
Micro local flash deals, 20, 101
Miso, 20
Mobile bar codes, 56
  design, 16–17, 17f, 21–23
  interface, 63, 67, 71
  literacy, 92
  touch, 57, 63, 76, 102
Mobile payment, 75–79, 77f, 79f, 102–103,
    103f

N
Near field communication (NFC), 76,
    78–79, 79f, 102
Neer, 16
NeoReader, 14
Nexus S 4G phones, 76–77
Nokia, 76

O
Offline usage, 64
Oink, 105
OPAC. *See* Library catalog (OPAC)

P
Page2RSS, 71
Path, 12, 20, 67, 86
Patrons
  connecting with, 42–44, 43f

location-based themes and trends, 20–21
promoting, 4, 46, 74–75
rewards, 4, 33–36, 33f, 46, 74–75, 81–83, 82f, 99
PayPal, 14, 76–79, 79f, 103f
PayPass, 77, 103f
Photo
    Instagram, 10, 12, 15, 15f, 20, 51, 104
    RSS and, 12, 67–71, 69f, 87
    sharing applications, 12, 15, 20, 67, 85, 86, 104
    stream, 12, 67–71, 69f, 87
Picasso, 86
Picplz, 12, 15, 20, 67, 86, 104
Pinterest, 105
Planning and developing, 11–14, 19, 20–23, 25–26, 101–105
Platforms, 4–5, 22, 32, 35, 50–51
Pocket Universe, 12, 15, 50, 51f
Privacy, 1–3, 5, 8, 27, 30, 32, 91–92
Prizes. See Rewards
Project management
    augmented reality, 47–55, 49f, 51f, 53f
    digital wallet and, 76, 78–79, 79f, 102
    Facebook page, 44–47
    Facebook Places, 44–45
    Foursquare, 29–40, 31f, 33f–34f, 38f–41f, 41–47, 43f, 90–93
    ideas, 63
    local recommendations, 71–75, 72f, 74f, 101–102
    location-based services, 62–63
    mobile payment, 75–79, 77f–79f, 102–103, 103f
    photo stream, 12, 15, 67–71, 69f, 85, 87, 104
    QR codes, 55–63, 56f, 58f, 60f–61f, 68–69, 69f, 84–86, 85f
    RSS feeds, 67, 70–71
    shelf reading, 15, 53–54, 53f
    social recommendations, 71–75, 72f, 74f
    staff training, 22–23, 26–27, 30, 47, 54, 77–78, 90–93
    strategic management, 21–23
    work flow assignments, 93
    See also Planning and developing

Promotion
    campaign, 27–28, 29–33
    Foursquare, 33–34, 33f, 35–38, 38f, 39–40, 39f, 81–83, 82f
    Gowalla, 63–67, 66f, 83–86, 85f
    hashtags, 15, 39, 52, 67–70, 69f, 86
    library administration and, 25–28
    prizes, 12, 23, 29–30, 33–36, 33f, 81–83, 82f
    QR code, 55–59, 56f, 58f, 60–63, 60f–61f, 84–86, 85f
    staff and, 26–28
    stakeholders and, 25–26
    URL, 62–63, 83, 97
    See also Marketing

Q
QR code
    bar codes, two-dimensional, 4, 12–13, 55, 57
    book reviews, 60–61, 61f–62f
    campaign, 55–59, 56f, 58f, 60–63, 60f–61f, 84–86, 85f
    code generating, 13–14, 55–57, 56f, 61–62
    digital wallet and, 76, 78–79, 79f, 102
    e-mail signatures, 56–57, 65, 84–85, 85f, 92
    embedded information, 55–57, 56f
    Facebook, 74, 83–84
    generators, 13–14
    Gowalla and, 63–67, 66f
    implications, 9–11
    Instagram account, 68–69, 69f
    library and, 59–61, 60f
    linking, 58–60, 62–63
    location-awareness services, 1, 3–5, 2f–3f, 5–8
    marketing, 84–86, 85f
    monitoring, 95–96, 96f, 97–99, 98f
    posting, 57–58, 58f
    readers, 14
    reference services, 61–62
    scanning, 4–5
    SMS message, 13–14, 58–59, 61–62
    social networks, 58–59
    staff training, 90–93
    testing, 57
    trends, 101–102

QR Droid, 14
QRStuff.com, 13, 56, 59–60
QuickMark, 14, 57

R

Radio Frequency Identification (RFID), 76
Rewards
  badges, 10, 38–40, 38f–39f
  Facebook, 84
  Foursquare, 12, 23, 29–30, 33–36, 33f
  Google's Offers program, 75
  Gowalla, 13, 63–67
  marketing, 83
  mayorships, 10, 12, 29, 31, 33–36, 33f,
    34f, 62, 83, 96
  micro, 10–11
  patrons, 4, 46, 74–75, 99
  prizes, 12, 23, 29–30, 33–36, 33f, 81–83,
    82f
  staff, 41–42, 92–93
  system, 37–38
  venue, 41–42
RSS feed, 12, 67–71, 69f, 87

S

Scavenger hunts, 42, 76
SCVNGR, 4, 16, 17f, 20
Service Set Identifier (SSID). See SSID
Shelf reading, 15, 53–54, 53f
Shelvar, 15, 53–54, 53f
Short message service (SMS). See SMS
  message
Smartphone
  apps, 11, 101–105, 105f
  bar codes, two-dimensional, 4, 12–13,
    55, 57
  Radio Frequency Identification (RFID),
    76
  template, 2
SMS message, 13–14, 58–59, 61–62
Social media
  Klout.com, 99
  linking, 58–59
  marketing and, 84–86
  recommendations, 71–75, 72f, 74f
  Twitter, 58
Social mechanics. See Promotion
SoundTracking, 20

Spot pages, 3, 10, 21, 64–68
Square card reader, 79, 79f
Squareup.com, 79, 79f
SSID, 13
Staff
  marketing to, 26–27
  rewards, 41–42, 92–93
  training, 22–23, 26–27, 30, 47, 54,
    77–78, 90–93
Stakeholders, 25–26
Stamps, 13, 67, 90
Starbucks, 35
Statistics. See Analytics; Metrics
Strategic management, 21–23
Symbian, 51–52
Synching accounts, 65

T

Tablets, 48, 92, 102
Tagging
  augmented reality, 48, 53–54, 86
  Facebook, 10
  friend, 3, 43, 46
  location-based services, 82, 102
  NFC, 79
  thematic, 66
  See also Hashtags
Technologies, 11–14, 21–23, 25–26,
  101–105
Texting, 13, 62
textPlus, 16, 17f
Thumbnails, 68
Titanium+Commerce, 78
Touch environment, 57, 63, 76, 102
Trends, 101–105, 103f, 105f
Tumblr, 68, 87, 97
Twitter
  Bizzy and, 73–74
  Gowalla, 65, 83
  direct message, 35
  hashtags, 52, 68–70, 69f
  Instagram, 68
  location-aware, 1, 4, 16, 20, 71
  marketing and, 74, 82–83, 86–87
  meme, 52
  patrons, 65
  QR code and, 14, 56, 58, 63, 86
  rewards, 35–36

social network link, 58–59
synching accounts, 65
tracking, 40, 97
Tweeps, 51
TwitPic, 86
Yfrog, 86

U
URL, 13, 70, 95
    linking, 58–59, 65
    marketing, 83
    shortening services, 14, 62–63, 97–98, 98f

V
vCalendar, 14, 60
vCard format, 14
Venue, 31–33, 31f, 33f
Verification code, 32, 33f

Video, 12, 14, 54, 59, 63
Vimeo.com, 48
Virginia Museum of Fine Arts, 48
Virtual Graffiti, 15, 49–50, 49f

W
Weather AR, 51
Whrrl, 16
Wi-Fi, 13–14, 37, 73
Wikipedia, 12, 51, 63

Y
Yahoo!, 65
Yelp, 4, 12, 14, 16, 20, 51–52
Yobongo, 16, 17f
YouTube, 14

Z
ZXing, 13, 56–57, 56f, 60

ABOUT THE AUTHOR

Joe Murphy is a Librarian and Technology Trend Spotter. He works as a consultant helping libraries and other industries prepare to meet upcoming technology shifts in the constantly evolving information landscape. Joe is an international keynote speaker, an author and editor, and a conference organizer. Joe worked at Yale as a Science Librarian from 2007 to 2011. He earned a master's degree in library and information science from the University of Hawaii in 2006 and a bachelor's degree in physics from Syracuse University. Joe enjoys sipping tea, traveling, poetry, practicing yoga, and checking in while doing all of the above. More information about Joe can be found on his website: http://joemurphylibraryfuture.com/. Connect with Joe on Twitter—@libraryfuture http://twitter.com/libraryfuture—and LinkedIn—http://www.linkedin.com/in/libraryfuture. And you can reach him by e-mail at libraryfuture@gmail.com.